"Brimming with witty and playful mockery, Shalev's story is also compassionate, an elegiac glimpse of the authentic pioneers of Zionist history. A genuine comic tour de force as well as a marvelous meditation on the mysterious workings of memory and the intricate tapestry of familial connections."
—*Forward*

"Probably one of the most enjoyable books ever written about obsessive-compulsive disorder."   —*Haaretz* (Israel)

"Lighthearted yet meaningful . . . As I read this, I felt like I was one of Shalev's cousins, sitting out behind his grandmother's house, listening to a great retelling of a story I knew by heart."
—*JewishBoston*

"Unfailingly charming . . . At once a mystery story, a fascinating glimpse into what life was like for the Labor Zionists of the early twentieth century, a moving family memoir, and, above all, a vivid, affectionate tribute to Grandma Tonia, who must now take her rightful place as one of history's most redoubtable matriarchs."   —*Words Without Borders*

"A loving and humorous family story about Israel's pioneers and their offspring."   —*Die Welt* (Germany)

"An unconventional and quite hilarious family scrapbook . . . Shalev's reflections on quirky uncles, family squabbles, the rich history of his Jewish heritage, and the legacy of the omnipresent American vacuum cleaner touch the heart and tickle the funny bone."   —*Kirkus Reviews*

*My Russian Grandmother and
Her American Vacuum Cleaner*

My
Russian Grandmother
and her American
Vacuum Cleaner

A Memoir

MEIR SHALEV

Translated from the Hebrew by
EVAN FALLENBERG

SCHOCKEN BOOKS · NEW YORK

Translation copyright © 2011 by Meir Shalev
All rights reserved. Published in the United States by Schocken Books,
a division of Penguin Random House LLC, New York, and distributed
in Canada by Penguin Random House of Canada, a division of Penguin
Random House Limited, Toronto. Originally published in hardcover in
the United States by Schocken Books, a division of Penguin Random
House LLC, New York, in 2011. Originally published in Israel as
Ha'davar Haya Kakha by Am Oved Publishers Ltd., Tel Aviv, in 2009.
Copyright © 2009 by Am Oved Publishers Ltd., Tel Aviv.

Schocken Books and colophon are
registered trademarks of Penguin Random House LLC.

Library of Congress Cataloging-in-Publication Data
Shalev, Meir.
[Davar hayah kakhah. English]
My Russian grandmother and her American vacuum cleaner : a memoir /
Meir Shalev ; translated from the Hebrew by Evan Fallenberg.
p.   cm.
ISBN 978-0-8052-1240-2 (paperback). ISBN 978-0-8052-4298-0 (ebook).
1. Shalev, Meir.   2. Authors, Israeli—20th century—Biography.
I. Title.
PJ5054.S384Z4613 2010   892.4'8609—dc22 [B]   2010033275

www.schocken.com
Cover images: (orange and lemon tree) missyoung/Shutterstock;
(donkey) Benguhan/Shutterstock; (woman and vacuum) CSA Images/
Getty Images

Cover design by Nayon Cho

Printed in the United States of America
First Paperback Edition
2 4 6 8 9 7 5 3 1

To my uncles and my aunts

*My Russian Grandmother and
Her American Vacuum Cleaner*

I

This is how it was: Several years ago, on a hot summer day, I rose from a pleasant afternoon nap and made a cup of coffee for myself, and while I stood sipping from the mug I noticed that everyone was looking strangely at me and holding back their laughter. When I bent down to put my sandals on I discovered the reason: my toenails, all ten of them, had been painted with shiny red nail polish.

"What is this?" I cried. "Who painted my toenails?"

From the other side of the porch door, which stood ajar, came the sound of giggling that I recognized at once from previous incidents.

"I know who did this," I said, raising my voice. "I'll find you and I'll catch you and I'll paint your noses and your ears with the very same shiny red polish you used on my toes, and I'll manage to do it all before my coffee turns cold!"

The giggles became laughter that confirmed my suspicions. While I lay sleeping, my brother's two little daughters, Roni and Naomi, had stolen in and painted my toenails. Later they would tell me that the younger of the two had done four nails while her older sister had done the other six. They had hoped I would not notice and that I would walk out in public, only to be scorned and ridiculed. But now that their scheme had been unmasked they burst into the room and pleaded: "Don't take it off, don't, it's really pretty."

I told them that I, too, thought it was really pretty, but that there was a problem: I had been invited to "an important event" where I was expected to speak, but I could not appear before the crowd with painted nails, since it was summer and in summer I wear sandals.

The girls said that they were familiar with both matters—the important event and my custom of wearing sandals—and that this was precisely the reason they had done what they did.

I told them that I would go to any other important event with shiny red toenails but not to this important event. And that was because of the crowd that would gather there, a crowd no sane man would appear before with painted toenails—and red ones, no less.

The event we were talking about was the inauguration of the old arms cache used by the Haganah, a Jewish paramilitary organization that operated in Palestine during the British Mandate. The cache had been built on a farm in the village of Nahalal and disguised to look like a cowshed cesspool. In my novel *The Blue Mountain* I had described an arms cache that never existed in a village that never existed in the Jezreel Valley, but my arms cache was also built and disguised exactly the same way. After the book was published, readers began to show up on the real farm in the real village, asking to see the real cache.

Rumor passed by word of mouth, the number of visitors grew and became a nuisance, and the owners of the property were smart enough to make the best of their situation. They renovated the cache, set up a small visitors' center, and thus added a new stream of income to their farm. That day, when my brother's two young daughters painted my toenails with red polish, was the day the renovated arms cache was being inaugurated, and I had been invited as one of the speakers at the ceremony.

"Now bring some nail polish remover and get this pretty stuff off me," I told Roni and Naomi. "And please hurry up because I have to get going already!"

The two refused. "Go like that!" they said.

I sat down and explained to them that this was a particularly manly event, that there would be generations of fighters from the Jezreel Valley in attendance, elders from the Haganah, the Israel Defense Forces, and the Palmach. Men of the sword and the plowshare, men who had bent spears into pruning shears and vice versa. In short, girls, these were people who would not react favorably to men with red polish on their toenails.

But Naomi and Roni paid no attention to my pleas. "What do you care?" they cried. "You said yourself it's pretty."

"If you don't take it off I'll wear shoes!" I threatened. "Nobody will see your red nail polish, and that'll be that!"

"You're afraid!" they exclaimed. "You're afraid what they'll say about you in the village."

Those words took effect at once. Without knowing it the two little girls had hit a soft underbelly. Anyone familiar with members of the old-time collective agricultural movement, anyone who has been upbraided by them, knows that in small villages eyes take everything in and comments are made with regularity and rumors take off and land like cranes in a sown field. All the more so in places whose pedigree is famed and illustrious, like Nahalal's. Here, the standards are more stringent, and anyone who leaves the path of the straight and narrow, who veers left or right, up or down—even a single mistake made in one's childhood—is not forgotten. Especially someone considered odd, eccentric, meshugah, or an underachiever, which is the complete opposite of *mutzlach,* one of the loftiest expressions of excellence the village bestows upon its most fortunate sons and daughters, those blessed with wisdom, industriousness, leadership qualities, and community spirit.

But after many years in the city the combination of the words "what" and "they'll say about you" and "in the village" had lost some of their power and threat. So I reconsidered and

5

decided to take up the gauntlet or, more accurately, the sandals. I put them on, thrust the notes for the speech I had prepared into my pocket, and set out for the inauguration of the old arms cache with my red-painted toenails exposed. The entire household eyed me—some with mirth, others with regret, some with schadenfreude, others with suspicion: Would I return to be reunited with my home and family? And in what condition?

Here I must admit and confess that despite my display of courage upon leaving the house, I became more and more anxious the closer I got to the event. By the time I arrived at the site I was absolutely beside myself. I silently prayed that no one would notice my toes, and my prayers were answered. No one made a single comment, nobody said a thing. On the contrary, everyone was warm and cordial. My hand was crushed by bold handshakes, my shoulder bent by manly slaps on the back. Even my short speech went off well and pleased the crowd—or so it seemed to me.

Naturally, I made metaphorical use of the arms cache as an image of memory and what is hidden in the depths of a person's soul. In the manner of writers, I prattled on about that which is above the surface and that which is below, that which the eye sees and that which it does not, and from there it was a short road to the tried-and-true literary merchandise of "reality" and the "relationship between truth and fiction in belles lettres" and a lot of other fodder that writers blithely use to sell their wares.

After I had finished speaking and descended from the small stage and was able to breathe in relief, one of the daughters of the family on whose property the arms cache had been built approached and asked to exchange a few words with me in private. She thanked me for my speech and said it had been just fine, but then, almost as an afterthought, she added that she wished to know which nail polish was my favorite. She said she very much liked the shade of red I used, as did two friends of hers sitting in the audience who had asked her to find out.

And as that same shade of red flushed across my cheeks, the young woman hastened to add that she herself had no problem with it, that she even found it rather nice, something she had always felt was missing in the village and could be a happy harbinger of things to come. However, to others in the audience my appearance at the event had raised some reservations.

"I thought no one had noticed," I said.

"Not noticed? It's all anyone's been talking about," she said. "But take consolation in the fact that no one was surprised. I even heard someone say, 'What do you want from the guy? He got it from Tonia. She was crazy in just the same way. That's the way it is in their family.'"

2

Tonia was my grandmother, my mother's mother, and in my eyes she was not at all crazy. She was different. She was distinctive. She was what we call a "character." She was not an easy person, and that's putting it mildly. But crazy? No. However, as in other matters, not everyone agrees with me. Other people have different opinions, both in the village and in the family.

The story I am about to tell here deals with my grandmother and her "sweeper." That is what we call the vacuum cleaner sent to her by Uncle Yeshayahu, the older brother of Grandpa Aharon, her husband. From the outset I wish to make it known that I am aware that "sweeper" and "vacuum cleaner" are two different appliances, but Grandma Tonia called her vacuum cleaner "the sweeper," so from that day until this very day we call every vacuum cleaner by the same name, using the same accent—her rolling Russian *r* and her deep Russian *ee*.

As for Uncle Yeshayahu, I never met him, but from childhood I heard stories about him that attested to his problematic, if not negative and harmful, personality. In the days of the Second Aliyah, prior to World War I, when Jewish pioneers were draining the swamps and settling the land, Uncle Yeshayahu chose to emigrate to America and make the desert of Los Angeles bloom instead. And to make matters worse, he changed his name to Sam, set himself up in business, and made money by exploiting the hard work of the proletariat.

The two brothers were sons of a Hasidic family and both left religion. But while Grandpa Aharon converted to another fervent faith, that of Socialism and Zionism, his older brother found his place in the world of American capitalism. Grandpa Aharon never forgave him for that. He even called him "the double traitor" for being neither a Socialist nor a Zionist.

As for the sweeper itself, it was a large and powerful vacuum cleaner made by General Electric, the likes of which had never before been seen in our village, in the Jezreel Valley, or in all of Palestine—nor has such an appliance ever been seen since. That is what my mother told me, still astounded by it at the telling. It sported a chrome-topped canister, huge and sparkling, she said, and large, silent rubber wheels and a strong electric motor and a thick and flexible suction tube. Still, with all the respect and affection I have for it, and in spite of the fact that the vacuum cleaner is the hero of this story, I must admit right now, up front, that this story is not one of our family's most important. It is not a love story, though it contains love. It is not a story of death, though quite a number of the story's heroes have passed away. It is not a story of treason and revenge, though both can be found in it. And it does not play host to the pain of other family stories, connected though it is by the suffering found therein as well.

In short, this is not one of the stories that wakes up with us, walks about with us, and stays with us, until we lie down, but rather a story that we tell to one another in pleasant circumstances, passing it from the first generation to those that did not know Grandpa Aharon or the sweeper sent by his brother to Grandma Tonia, or even Tonia herself.

Perhaps I will write the extended story of my extended family in another book at another time. I will tell of my parents and their parents, of all the Jabbok streams they crossed and the squabbles they squabbled. I will describe the hard labor their bodies endured and the incarcerations their hearts suffered. I will rouse my pen to the duels of love, the ideological power struggles, the championships of affliction, the fights for control over the wells of memory. I will name the well-known lunatics and the unknown lunatics. I will write about the abducted daughter and the deposed sons—and all this, ladies and gentlemen, as part and parcel of the Zionist revolution.

If I do write that book it will not be today or tomorrow or in the coming years. I will write it when I am older and bolder, more forgiving and more temperate. And even this promise I do not promise to keep. In the meantime, in this slight book, I wish to tell one story only: that of Grandma Tonia and her sweeper, which Uncle Yeshayahu sent from the United States.

The story, as I have already mentioned, is a true story, its heroes real and their names real. But as with all its brethren in our family, this story, too, has several versions, each one containing exaggerations and additions and deletions and augmentations. And there is one more thing I need to say, a sort of explanation for what is to come: here and there I will add a small side story, one that is necessary for comprehension and orientation; I will rouse a forgotten affair from its slumber, summoning images from the beyond. Here and there a chuckle will replace a moan and tears will give way to laughter.

3

My grandfather on my mother's side, Aharon Ben-Barak, was born in 1890 and grew up in the town of Makarov in Ukraine. He was nineteen years old when he came to Palestine and, like many of his friends, pioneers of the Second Aliyah, he wandered the country and passed through many places: Zichron Yaacov and Hulda, Ben Shemen and Kfar Uriah, Be'er Yaacov—which he and Grandma Tonia pronounced "Beryakov"—and other farms and colonies. Because he passed from place to place and had observant eyes and a sensitive heart and a sense of humor and a talent for writing, he published occasional articles and reports in a broadsheet called *The Young Laborer*.

His first wife, Shoshanna Pekker, from the village of Rokitno in Ukraine, bore him two sons: Itamar, my oldest uncle, and Binyamin, whom everyone called Binya. In 1920 Shoshanna contracted malaria and died young. Three years later several other family members came to Palestine from Rokitno: Shoshanna's half brother Yaacov and half sister Tonia, along with their mother, Batya. The father of the family, Mordechai Zvi, had come earlier and died, and Tonia's older brothers Moshe and Yitzhak were already living here.

Aharon Ben-Barak, widower and father of two small children, and Tonia Pekker, an eighteen-year-old maiden, decided to marry. Many years later, after I had joined the family and had grown up and become one of the people before whom she

The family in the courtyard, Nahalal, 1925

poured the bitter words from her bitter heart, Grandma Tonia would tell me again and again her version of the story of their marriage: "This is how it was: I was a young girl who did not know the ways of the world and he was experienced, older than me by fourteen years, and he made me promises and he told me stories, and this is what happened . . ."

"This is how it was": these were the words she always used for beginning any story she told. She pronounced them in her thick Russian accent. Her children—my mother, her brothers and sister—also said "This is how it was," with the same accent, when they began a story. And not only they. To this very day, we all use this opening and that accent when we want to say "This is the truth. What I am about to tell is precisely what happened."

There are those who say that Grandpa Aharon did in fact fall in love with Grandma Tonia the moment he caught sight of her as she alighted from the ship. There are those who whisper that, as is de rigueur in Russian novels, he even threatened to kill himself if she did not respond to his wooing. Grandma Tonia herself made that claim, adding that Grandpa Aharon even said he would throw himself into the Jordan River. Why the Jordan River? Well, hanging oneself is not suited to this sort of suicide. Sleeping pills and tall buildings were unavailable. Pistols (which they pronounced "pissles") were hard to come by and ammunition was rare and expensive; a person who wasted a bullet on taking his own life was therefore guilty of egoism and doomed to social condemnation. And then there was the Jordan: poetic, romantic, not as large as the rivers they had in Russia but with an aura all its own. What's more, it was nearby and convenient; "In the Land of Israel everything is close," Grandpa Aharon himself told me many years later, during a conversation in which he denied everything that Grandma Tonia had said about this incident.

Others related that Grandpa Aharon had wanted Grandma Tonia for a simpler and more practical reason: he hoped she would raise the two small boys her sister had borne him and be a good mother to them. But that did not happen; Grandma Tonia's relationship with Shoshanna's sons is an open wound in our family history. Shoshanna and Tonia were also born to their father and two different mothers, causing some to claim that after two generations of second marriages and children from two mothers, the matter is far more complicated than anything I have tried to describe up to this point.

As stated, Grandpa Aharon was a Second Aliyah pioneer while Grandma Tonia came during the Third Aliyah, in the early twenties. He was among the "founders of Nahalal" while she was considered "an early settler of Nahalal." However, in spite of these differences, to which members of the oldest moshavim and kibbutzim attach huge importance, they managed to bring five children into the world: Micha, Batya—my mother—the twins Menahem and Batsheva, and Yair, the child of their old age. All five were born with a talent for storytelling, and many of those stories were about their mother.

"She arrived from Russia," my mother told me about Tonia, "a young woman with her hair in braids and wearing a high school girl's uniform, drinking her tea like this, with her pinky finger extended alongside the glass, and she came straight to the valley, to the dust and dirt and hard work and mud . . ."

I sensed she wished to understand and explain her, maybe even forgive her for something: "She came here, discovered that all the promises of property owned by her father were untrue, that Grandpa Aharon, who had many virtues and talents, was no great farmer, and she sank into a life of labor and deprivation. And yet, she made up her mind not to be broken, not to return to Russia or desert to America or run off to Tel Aviv. We didn't have an easy time of it with her, but the entire family has her to thank for this farm."

Indeed, Grandpa Aharon was inclined toward things other than agriculture. I have already related that on occasion he penned reports and articles for *The Young Laborer* and in Nahalal he wrote and edited a satirical bulletin called *The Mosquito*. The Seder nights he organized were renowned. After families finished their individual Seders at home they would gather in the village hall, where he would lead a riotous Seder of his own, with stinging send-ups of people and events from the village and the movement that he wrote himself, all to the tune of songs from the Passover Hagaddah.

However, the next morning he still had to wake up and continue plowing and milking and sowing and reaping, and it happened on occasion that he could no longer endure the responsibility and the burden, and Grandpa Aharon would announce that his head hurt and then he would run off, and Grandma Tonia would say, "He's 'runoff' again," and she would chase him down and bring him back.

"It was a tragedy for him and for her," my mother told me. "My father should have lived a different life in a different place. A life more suited to his personality and his talents. But she was determined to hang on to the farm by the skin of her teeth, and she sank those teeth into the earth and into the house and into us and into him. And since every person needs an enemy, hers was dirt."

4

The first Nahalal settlers lived in tents, after which they moved to wooden huts; the first proper buildings erected were for the animals, not the people. Only in 1936—fifteen years after Nahalal was established—were homes built for the farmers and the village wired for electricity. This fact has great importance since the main character of the story, of any story, must take action. And the main character of this particular story is an electrical appliance, the vacuum cleaner.

Each family inaugurated its home as it saw fit. I do not know what other families did, but Grandma Tonia arranged a small and special ceremony whose meaning and influence was not understood by all: she wrapped the handle of the front door with a small rag. The house was new and clean, she explained, and the handle was new and shiny, and the rag was meant to keep it from getting stained or dirty.

Everyone laughed, but within a few days it became clear that that little rag, seemingly so innocent, was itself a kind of pioneer. Other rags followed, each placed on a handle of every door in the house and on some of the drawer handles as well, and those of the windows and cupboards. The rags remained there until their—and her—final day.

Grandma Tonia placed another rag over her left shoulder. This rag was larger than all its brothers: it was aware of its own importance and primacy, a kind of guard rag that accompanied her everywhere she went and was meant for immediate intervention—say she needed to blot out a speck of dirt that had escaped her notice and was suddenly discovered, or she happened upon some implement that needed cleaning, or she had to wipe her hands before she touched something clean that did not have a rag of its own.

Even I, who was born twelve years after the house was built, remember clearly her shoulder rag and all its comrades dangling from handles like little battle flags, protecting them from the touch of hands or fingers. In those days, working hands were praised and prized by one and all, the hands of the builder and the laborer and the guard and especially the farmer, as they planted and reaped and milked and harvested. Grandma Tonia, too, was a hardworking farmer and her hands labored at every chore, but she was also a realistic woman, and she knew that with all due respect to farmwork in general and, specifically, to labor carried out by Zionist pioneering hands, the hands of a farmer touched every kind of dirt: mud and dust, cow dung and chicken dung, the "black lotion" applied to trees and the black grease used on machines. And all this pretty stuff was merely looking for a clean place to stick to and make filthy. Even if a person washed his hands well, he left spots, or worse: permanent stains.

At the time, the house consisted of three rooms plus a kitchen and a bathroom and a front door that faced the street and a back door that faced the yard. Concrete was poured by the back door to form what we called "the platform," and it was on this wide slab that most family business was conducted. I had not been born yet, and later the stories about the platform would fill me with envy. This is where they sat and talked, where they shucked corn and peeled potatoes, where they plucked and quartered pigeons and chickens, where they kneaded dough and let stories rise, where they pickled cucumbers, preserved fruit, made jams. This is also where Uncle Yitzhak, Grandma Tonia's brother, dismantled the vacuum cleaner sent by Uncle Yeshayahu, discovering its secrets and its shame, but we shall come to that—everything in its time.

The jams simmered in a large copper basin passed from house to house in the village and placed on a bonfire in the yard. At our house the bonfire burned in the shade of the pomegranate tree next to the platform, and the jams kept for a very long time in their sealed jars. One day, many years after Grandma Tonia's death, I found such a jar in the old wooden hut and opened it with a can opener. A wisp of bonfire smoke rose from it and, as happens with bonfire smoke, it caused my eyes to tear.

Some fifteen years after the house was built it was enlarged and renovated. The old kitchen became an additional bedroom, a new kitchen was built atop the platform, and next to it a covered porch, along with a shower and toilet. This is the house as I came to know it. I remember it well, inside and out, and I recall how Grandma Tonia looked after it zealously.

First of all, she insisted that people enter through the back door and never the front, because if a guest came in through the front door he would find himself in the preserved and forbidden part of the house. Every time someone knocked at the front door, her resolute cry issued from inside the house: "Around back! Come in the second door!" and the guest would have to circle the house—without letting his foot step onto earth from the paved pathway, thereby bringing in mud or dust—only to find that here, too, he could not enter unless he was a particularly important and special visitor.

Grandma Tonia liked having guests, but her "house-pitality" did not include actually allowing guests into the house; she preferred entertaining outside. Visitors sat on the porch and Grandma Tonia would bring out glasses of tea, cookies with jam centers, fruit. They no doubt wondered what was inside the house that made her guard it so carefully. The lucky few who were granted permission to enter in fact found a modest and completely ordinary home with a small kitchen on the right side, a hallway ending at a shower and toilet, and a "dining room" on the left side. I put dining room in quotes because it was that only in name. The room was used for dining just once a year, for the Seder night. The rest of the time it was slept in, and meals were eaten on the porch or in the kitchen.

From the dining room another small hallway veered off and led to the older part of the house. It was here, my mother told me, that the family had first lived, after years in the hut. Her eyes shone when she spoke about it. It was a house full of life and activity and song and humor. But when Grandma and Grandpa's children grew up and moved out, that wing was closed off for good, and that is how I remember it—sealed off and forbidden. This wing had a room for select and special guests and two rooms completely out of bounds to all humankind, including family members and even "relations of blood" (Grandma Tonia differentiated between "relations of blood" and "relations of no blood"). But this, too, is not part of the story I am trying to tell here, the story of a vacuum cleaner sent to her by her brother-in-law from America.

Here, in these two locked rooms, she kept her "furnishings." To the reader picturing mahogany and ebony, commodes and cabinets, I must say that this was the simplest of furniture: there was a cupboard that I am tempted to call the "holy ark" but will not. There was a sofa upon which no person ever stretched out and two small armchairs in which no person ever sat, a sideboard with drawers and doors that remained unopened and in which could be found cutlery that knew no table or diner. As a child I suspected that this cutlery lived only in the minds of my mother and her sister, Batsheva, and since in our family memory and imagination are two names for the same thing, I doubted their existence. However, after Grandma Tonia's death I saw them with my own eyes.

In the adjacent room there was a double bed with a tall metal headboard painted dark brown to resemble wood. In the past it had served as Grandma and Grandpa's bed, but in my day no one slept in it. It felt neither the weight nor the heat of any body, not the tossing and turning of the restless sleeper, not the hum of a dreamer or the thrum of lovers—"The bed knew love when there was love," as one relative put it deftly—and not the touch of a blanket or sheet other than the one used to cover it and protect it from dust.

Not only the bed, but all its cellmates—the armchairs and the regular chairs and the sofa and the table and the cupboard and the sideboard—were draped in such old-sheet shrouds. No person reclined on them, no eyes beheld them other than those of Grandma Tonia, who entered there in order to "pass a rag" over them and ensure that none was dirty or had escaped. But once a year, in honor of the Seder night, the regular chairs were removed and brought to the dining room, which is how I was allowed to visit the holy of holies, for it was prior to Passover in my eighth year of life that I was deemed mature enough and responsible enough to be called upon to help with the holiday preparations.

I remember that day quite clearly. I stood behind Grandma Tonia, curious and excited. She inserted the key and turned it, opened the door, and said, "You are permitted to enter, but do not touch anything."

I entered, my first time in her forbidden rooms. As I write these words I recall my last time in those rooms as well, some thirty years later, when we came down from the cemetery to the house after burying her. But back then she was alive and she opened the locked door with a key she had fished from her pocket.

A cool silence, dim and limpid, greeted me. The air inside had been standing so long that it felt to my skin like water. The windows and shutters were closed. The rags that protected the handles had nearly disintegrated with age, as if woven like lace. Everything was white and clear and slack and clean, so clean that two sunrays that had found their way through cracks in the shutters encountered no motes of dust as they did in other rooms; they merely left two spots of trembling light on the wall.

Grandma Tonia removed the covering from one of the chairs that stood in the corner. It blinked its wooden eyes, exposed and blinded.

"Can you take it to the dining room?" she asked me.

"Yes," I said.

"On your own?"

"Yes."

"Lift it up. Don't drag it across the clean floor on me and don't scritch me the walls with it."

In addition to the richness and the literariness and the accent, her Hebrew had another characteristic: every verb was directed at herself. Chairs were dragged on her, clean sidewalks were dirtied on her, painted walls were scritched on her. "Scritch" is an old family verb still current in our dictionary of expressions and idioms. It is derived from the Yiddish word for "scratch," but we use it only for describing scratches on walls.

A language must describe many worlds: the realistic world

in which it lives and works, and the frightening, wishful, imaginary worlds in which it and the people who speak it would like or not like to live. In many realistic houses in that realistic period of time, hallway walls and dining-room walls and kitchen walls were painted with oil paint some five feet high so they could be washed. Grandma Tonia, who fulfilled the wall-washing commandment on a daily basis, considered a scratch in the oil paint to be such grave damage that she gave it its own name: scritch.

Taking the greatest care not to scritch a single scritch, I brought the chair to the dining room for her and placed it there for her. It looked around, uncomfortable in its sudden nakedness and the freedom and the strong light, so exposed and so near to the simple chairs that had arrived from the porch and the kitchen. The latter were accustomed to the light and the company, to being looked at and touched, and they told joyful, gossipy stories among themselves—so said my mother—about all kinds of rear ends they had happened to meet, while the locked-room chair was pleased and satisfied at being let out into the open and liberated, though he knew it was for only one night and that he was destined to meet only a single rear end, and that after Seder night he would be cleaned with a large brush, washed with soap and water, then dried and finally wrapped in his old sheet and returned to his prison until the next Passover, the Holiday of Freedom.

5

I mentioned before that in Grandma Tonia's house there were two bathrooms, the old one and the new. In the new one there was only a shower, but in the old one there was a real bath as well. When her children were still at home it was in use, but once they had grown up and moved away it was closed off forever.

Bathrooms, my mother explained to me, are shifty rooms and very dangerous. Strangely enough, it is bathrooms—whose main purpose is cleanliness—that are astonishing in their capacity for making dirt and getting dirty: the tiles, the floor, the faucets, the various sanitary appliances. You don't need to be a genius to understand that people who use showers are dirty, otherwise they would not have any use for the shower. And a person that dirty enters the shower and leaves behind him all the filth he wishes to remove from his body. He drips turbid water on the clean floor, he smudges the clean tiles with his fingers, and he leaves all sorts of stains and marks behind him.

In winter the family bathed in the house, but in summer, outside—the adults in an "excellent shower," as Grandma Tonia called it, which was nothing more than a sort of pipe that ran alongside the wall of the cowshed. Children, on the other hand, bathed in the "trough," which I shall explain later. Over the years, the bathing conditions improved: next to the chick run a laundry house was set up where there was actually hot running water, thanks to a huge chimney boiler. At first, pruned tree branches and dried ears of corn were burned there, but later a device was installed that dripped oil, drop by drop. I can still bring to mind the sound of the unique way it burned, a sort of dull and mysterious roar that was nothing like any other sound and very pleasant to the ear of a child while at the same time frightening.

As with every other home, there was, in Grandma Tonia's house, a half bathroom known as the "restroom." In spite of its name, however, people were not invited to rest there. According to one version of my father's first visit to the family home in Nahalal, when he was courting my mother, he naively entered

21

the restroom and found it spotlessly clean. The toilet seat was down, and on top of it a newspaper was spread, on top of which was placed a wooden board, and on top of that another newspaper on which stood a *wundertopf* that held a stovetop plum cake in the process of cooling.

This is the place to mention two things. The first is that Grandma Tonia was a wizard at anything made with plums: her plum cake and plum jam were works of art. The second is that my father was called more than once in the village a "tiligent" and a "tilignat"—words used by the villagers to describe city folk who wore glasses and read and wrote books instead of working. Still, some of the tiligents and tilignats were actually intelligent, and my father understood that the restroom of his future mother-in-law was not designed for its initial purpose. So instead of carrying through with his plan he held it in and reached for the cake, eating half of it before exiting the restroom with an innocent look on his face. The matter did not improve relations between them, but I will get to that later.

I, too, had an incident with the restroom. When I was four or five years old and staying at her house, Grandma Tonia caught me by the restroom door and demanded to know where, in my opinion, I was headed.

"Here," I said, pointing at the closed door, not comprehending the problem.

"Do you have to do number one or number two?" she asked.

"Number one."

She breathed a sigh of relief, told me I could do that outside, and at once steered me, gently but forcefully—Grandma Tonia was short of stature but very strong—out the door and into the yard, where she explained that next to the cowshed there was an old outhouse from the days in which the family had lived in a hut, and if I wanted I could also use the sluice that carries away the muck from the cows or I could water the special citrus tree that Grandpa had planted and grafted, about which I shall also tell later on.

"And don't go there empty-handed," she said, handing me a small bag of rubbish. "If you're going out anyway, then take this with you and toss it into the muck."

Grandma Tonia could not stand dirt anywhere inside or near the house, even if it had already been collected and bagged and thrown into the trash bin, whose very purpose was to contain it. Anyone heading out back got some garbage from her wrapped in a newspaper or an old paper bag from the village store, and often she added a request: "Returning back, bring a few eggs from the chickens."

"Don't go empty-handed" and "returning back" were her standard instructions, and they meant: don't just walk about aimlessly, strolling in the fields, gazing at the view. This is a farm and there is a lot of work to be done and there is always something to take, to bring, to move from one place to another, to toss out, to hand over.

I took-out-for-her the garbage, went-into-for-her the yard, and watered-for-her Grandpa's special citrus tree on the way, while Grandma hastened to the restroom door, inspected the handle I had already touched, wiped it clean with the large rag thrown over her shoulder, resettled the small rag that belonged there, and closed the door.

This is how I remember her syntax and her house, whether by her self-directed verbs or the "second door" around back or the covered front porch with the wraparound bench or the kitchen and dining room, the hall painted with oil paint and the closed doors of the rooms. More than once I asked my mother what was behind all those doors with all the rags dangling from the handles. She explained that "here is the shower one may not shower in and here is the restroom one may not rest in and here are the bedrooms one may not bed down in, and here," she said, standing beside the old bathroom, the Holy of Holies, the sanctuary, where there was a real bathtub, "here is where the vacuum cleaner lives, her sweeper."

"Her sweeper?" I asked expectantly and with joy, because my mother pronounced the word just as her mother did—"svieeperrr"—turning the *w* into a *v* and deepening the two *e*'s and clicking her tongue against the roof of her mouth so that the English *r* became a Russian *rrr*. Such an imitation brought joyful connotations, a story hiding just beyond view. And not just one of the same old stories that she and her siblings always told me about prancing horses and flying donkeys and the neighbors' grandfather who was so small he rode rabbits at night, but a wondrous story about a mysterious creature called the "sweeper" who was imprisoned in the forbidden bathroom in Grandma's house, right here behind the locked door.

"Tell me about him."

"About her sweeper? What's there to tell about a vacuum cleaner?"

"Tell me, please. Please!"

"It's a vacuum cleaner that Uncle Yeshayahu sent her from America."

"America?" I repeated, dumbfounded. America did not appear regularly in family stories.

"Yes, from America. Los Angeles, California, U.S.A."

That required a deep breath. So many important names, forbidden and alluring, in one single sentence.

6

And another deep breath. Not only for that moment, when the word "America" made an appearance in my mother's stories for the first time, and not only for that place, Nahalal, where America meant such different and contrasting things, but also a deep breath for here and now, years after the fact, as the matter is recalled and written.

The America of then and there, of my childhood in the village, was both a land of enchantment and an enemy nation. The most powerful tractors and the finest-quality harvesters came from America. The RIDGID pipe wrench—"The best wrench in the world, with a full lifetime warranty," Uncle Menahem and Uncle Yair would exclaim—came from there, as did the almighty Jeep that could travel anywhere, and the mighty tommy gun that Uncle Micha and Uncle Itamar had used during the War of Independence and spoke of with awe and reverence.

And there's more: The settlers of the Wild West were pioneers like our grandmothers and grandfathers. The May First International Workers' Day came from America. A large number of the soldiers who defeated the Nazis were American. The great American agronomist Luther Burbank, developer of the Santa Rosa plum and the father of potato-seed planting (as opposed to using cuttings), was American. The book about his life, *The Harvest of the Years,* was very popular among the Jewish villages and farms of the time, and how miraculous was it that he lived in the very same California to which Uncle Yeshayahu had emigrated and started a business and changed his name to Sam instead of making aliyah to the Land of Israel?

For capitalism came from America, and hedonism, and vacuity and dandyism and makeup and luxuries and the music that my young uncle Yair listened to, to his father's consternation. In short, no one could understand how it was that the land that had given humanity the combine and corn and the three-point system for harnessing a tractor—one in back and the other two at the tips of the hydraulic arms—could be the perpetrator of a way of life so undesirable and absolutely futile.

I am not certain that America knew this, but in addition to the Soviet Union, East Germany, China, and North Korea, it had, during the days of my childhood, another rival. Not a large one, not a strong one, not a particularly dangerous one, if truth be told, but a bitter, moralistic, and determined foe if ever there was one: a number of moshavim and kibbutzim in the Land of Israel.

We're talking about a level of animosity that lasted for years—so long, in fact, that even I, two generations away from the founding of the village, was witness to it. Once, in the early sixties, an Israeli singing duo called the Mandrakes—Israel Gurion and Benny Amdursky—came to Nahalal. At first they sang Israeli songs, then they moved to Russian ballads, and as a finale they sang an American song. It was a pleasant, innocent folksong by The Weavers, if I'm not mistaken, or perhaps by Pete Seeger alone, but as far as the villagers were concerned this was an unforgivable sin. An American song¿ Sung in English¿! At once, several of the old-timers rose to their feet and shouted, "Not here! Not in Nahalal!" and they would not let the singers continue.

The nail-polishing with which I started this story was an American evil as well, an evil of unparalleled proportions that had infiltrated the Land of Israel through pictures in newspapers and letters, and photographs sent by relatives, and motion pictures and rumors that had floated from there to here. The "manicure" had led astray not a few souls in places where the weak of character and the immoral could be found, like Tel Aviv, and in spite of the best efforts of the founders' generation, several victims could be counted even at Nahalal. And that is how the manicure found its way into the family lexicon of expressions and idioms, then made its way into the village lexicon and perhaps even that of the entire Jezreel Valley.

The exact expression, which we use to this very day, is "They say she gets manicures, too," which expresses a baseness, an absence of values, an ideological and spiritual downfall. The source of this expression was a conversation that took place around the dinner table in which someone pointed out that a certain member of the village had "sold melons to a trader passing by on the main road," which is to say that he had acted in contradiction to the principles of the moshav, which required all produce to be bought and sold through the official institutions. In those days this was a truly immoral crime, and it prompted someone else to add that "if that isn't bad enough, his wife is involved with someone from Ramat David"—not, heaven forbid, the neighboring kibbutz (the situation was not that out of control) but from the adjacent air force base.

And then, when it was clear to one and all that the family under discussion was damaged from every aspect and angle possible, that this was a family that had violated both the moshav's constitution and the moral code of mankind in its entirety, there came the final crush, like that given by a work boot to a miserable cigarette butt or cockroach in the yard, the line that underscored the lowest depravity to which one could sink: "They say she gets manicures, too."

Not that the contemptible relatives of the manicure—lipstick and mascara and powder and rouge—were accepted in the village; certainly not. But the manicure had been chosen as the most negative symbol of them all because it showed up on fingers, the fingers of those very same working hands whose purpose was to plow and dig and plant and build. Those pioneering hands that the revolution meant to detach from the quill pen and the commerce and the Talmudic debating, and return to weapons and tools and labor and farming. Hands that would hold pruning shears and squeeze udders, hands that would grasp the handle of a scythe and pull a trigger if necessary. So how could these be used for preening and beauty? Surely no one with manicured hands would agree to dirty her fingernails in the cowshed or in the field or chip them filling magazines with bullets. The only thing they were good for was coquetry, for being painted with red polish and shown off.

Grandpa Aharon did not stop with the Battle of the Manicure; he set out on a crusade against chewing gum as well—guilty of causing "pointless masticating," which was yet another degenerate Americanism, one he grouped together with such unwanted and unwarranted products and customs as sweets, neckties, taxis, and all other "luxuries," as he and his cronies referred to all bourgeois American pleasures and, in fact, any pleasure at all that extended beyond a glass of tea and "herring tails," which is what Grandpa Aharon called the whole herring.

Any time he caught one of his grandchildren chewing gum he scolded the guilty party: "Get that chinga out of your mouth at once!" "Chinga" was one of Grandpa Aharon's malapropisms, a mangling of "chewing gum," words he had heard from the mouths of the British soldiers who had served in the area during the period of the Mandate. I've been told that on occasion a few of them would appear in the yard asking to buy some of the cheese Grandma Tonia made so well, or to eat watermelon chilled in a wet bag she had hung in the shade of a tree, where it could catch a breeze, or, most important, to see a house in which lived children and a mother and a father, since they were far away from their own families. In gratitude they would slip tempting packs of chewing gum from their pockets, enraging Grandpa.

Like his friends, the other founders of the village, he too held up his trousers with a rope of straw. And in winter they all placed empty burlap sacks atop their heads and shoulders, one corner turned toward the other like a large monk's hood, in order to protect themselves from rain and as a show of proletarian modesty and making do with little.

In truth, Grandma Tonia enjoyed fixing herself up a little from time to time. She did not have her hands manicured or outline her eyes with kohl, but here and there she adorned her hair with a bourgeois ribbon or hair clip, and there were those who accused her of standing out in this as well. But she was a freethinker, and just as she ornamented herself from time to time, so too did she wear her work clothes according to her own style: there was always a kerchief on her head, that rag over her shoulder, and, during the scorching days of summer, she worked in the yard wearing one of Grandpa Aharon's gray sleeveless undershirts. More than once when I have spotted young girls these days wearing one of those undershirts and thinking they are quite daring and original I smile to myself, because it was my grandmother who invented this style a long, long time before they did.

When my mother told me that hiding behind the locked bathroom door was an American vacuum cleaner, I was stunned.

"From America?" I asked again, wondering whether in addition to the vacuum cleaner there were also trunks full of forbidden chinga, makeup, and rock 'n' roll records hiding behind the locked bathroom door in Grandma Tonia's house.

"Uncle Yeshayahu sent it to her," my mother told me. "But she has only ever used it once. Then she locked it away in here."

"Why?"

"It's a complicated story."

"And then what happened?"

"When?"

"When she locked it up. What happened next?"

"That's a long story, too," my mother said. "I'll tell it to you one day. In the meantime, don't mention the sweeper to anyone outside the family. It's a secret!"

Thus I began to understand what will become clear to the reader, too, as the story unfolds: The secrets of other families in the village had to do with embarrassing failures, stains on reputations, forbidden loves, psychiatric hospitalizations, cowardliness on the battlefield, criminal offenses, out-of-wedlock pregnancies, luxuries, and selling melons to passing merchants on the main road. But in our family such exhilarating secrets were quite rare, and if they existed at all they were spread like figs dried by the sun, exposed to one and all. Our mysterious secret was really a large American vacuum cleaner sent from Los Angeles, California, by the double traitor—a non-Zionist and a non-Socialist—to his sister-in-law on the first workers' moshav established by the pioneers of the Second Aliyah in the Land of Israel. Grandma Tonia's sweeper, which had been sentenced to life imprisonment in her bathroom with its locked and bolted door guarded by a revolving sword in the shape of a rag placed on the handle.

7

Back in those days, all the village children took part in the hard work, shouldering the burden in the cowshed and the orchard and the yard and the chicken coop and the field. But Grandma Tonia's two daughters—my mother, Batya, and my aunt, Batsheva—were doubly enslaved because they were required to share the household cleaning chores as well. For this, too, Grandma had a special expression of warning against attempts at mutiny or evasion, a threat we use to this very day: "I'll take chunks out of you!"

Every morning she woke them up very early so that before going to school they could manage to clean. And to ensure they got their work done she would move the hands of the wall clock by an hour. Thus, Tonia's daughters would arrive at school at nine o'clock instead of eight, fatigued after several hours of work.

Their schoolteacher, Shmuel Pinneles, asked Grandma Tonia to come to school. He demanded an explanation and she did not bother to make denials.

"They have to help clean the house," she informed him.

She was not the only villager to keep children at home to help with chores, and the teacher grew angry and scolded her as he did other parents. "They are schoolgirls!" he said. "They need to study! They must arrive at school on time and not fall asleep in the classroom because they are so tired."

My grandmother rose to her feet, pulled her foreshortened body as tall as it would go in order to show that his time was up—there was a lot of work to do—and she left. Pinneles sighed. He could not have imagined what would happen.

Several weeks later, on a Friday morning, two hours before the end of the school day, there was a knock at the classroom door. Before he could even say "Come in," the door opened. Grandma Tonia stood in the doorway. The children with mothers who were not Grandma Tonia took no pains to hide their smiles. My mother shrank in her chair.

"Good morning," Pinneles said. He started to add "And to

31

what do we owe your visit here this morning?" but Grandma Tonia cut him off.

"Today is Friday!" she proclaimed.

"Absolutely true," the teacher affirmed as if responding to a pupil who had answered a question correctly.

The children, other than my mother, snickered to one another. Here and there even a peal of laughter could be heard.

"There is a lot of work to do before the Sabbath!" she announced.

"Here in the classroom we work hard, too," Pinneles said.

"Batya needs to come home to help me clean."

"We are in the middle of a lesson now," the teacher told her. "Batya will return home in the afternoon, like all the other children, when school has finished."

Grandma Tonia marched into the classroom. Her eyes moved from the teacher to her daughter. My mother gathered her belongings into her cloth rucksack and stood up from her chair.

"I have to help her," she told the teacher, not by way of asking permission but as an explanation, and even perhaps as a statement of fact about the way the world works: the sun shines in the morning, rivers flow to the sea, stars follow their paths, and I must clean.

Pinneles sighed a sigh similar to the one he had sighed at his previous meeting with Grandma Tonia, and did not say a word. Grandma Tonia walked out of the classroom, leaving the door open. Batya followed her and closed it.

Did she walk beside her mother or far behind? Did she plod along after her or run ahead in anger? And what did she say to her on their way home? Maybe she said nothing, preferring silence? Maybe she took a different route, strangling her tears and spilling her words only in the depths of her heart? I do not know the answers. I did not hear this story from her but from

Grandmother and mother

Penina Gary, her good friend, her "classmate," as they called each other then.

"I couldn't understand," Penina told me, "how it was that Batyaleh didn't refuse, didn't even argue. Usually your mother had a smart answer for everything and she knew how to stand up for herself."

I imagine she behaved that way for the same reason she did not mention the story of her mother's visit to school at all: she was ashamed, or worse, ashamed of her shame. But the matter has other facets as well. Nahalal at the time was a place of renown and pride, held in esteem by Jewish pioneers across the Land of Israel and even more so in the eyes of the villagers themselves. And in the manner of such places, once the residents were done ranking Tel Aviv and Jerusalem, New York and the neighboring moshav of Kfar Yehoshua in comparison to their own village, they began judging and ranking one another. Thus it was that my mother did not want to wage an argument with her mother in front of her friends, to put ammunition in the hands of the mockers and the slanderers. She simply rose from her chair, left the classroom, and went home to clean.

And there was what to clean. She and her sister Batsheva shook carpets and blankets and bedspreads—far from the house, of course, so the wind would not blow the dust in through the windows—and they washed the pavement, one sister spraying with the hose and the other scrubbing the cement with a large, tough-bristled brush. Then after that, the crowning glory: the daily washing of the floors.

I do not know in what year the cleaning implement known as a squeegee was born, but it never gained admittance to Grandma Tonia's house, for it was not enough that the squeegee leaves marks on the floor or that it doesn't clean corners and baseboards "as they should be cleaned": by its very nature it is an implement used by deniers and the lazy, by people who abstain from bending to the floor of reality and investigating it from up close. That is why my mother and her sister held rags in their hands, bent to the floor, and washed it every day, repeating the process again and again until Grandma Tonia was satisfied with the results.

"And when was she satisfied?" my mother asked like an experienced storyteller who is in the habit of asking when the listener is familiar with the story.

"When?" I repeated, just as the experienced listener must respond when he and the experienced storyteller both know the answer.

And indeed, Grandma Tonia was satisfied only when the rinse water soaked into the rag and squeezed into the bucket was completely clean and clear. And in order to determine this, she checked them "good good": she scooped a little water from

34

the bucket into the palm of her hand and brought it to the light. If the water was not as clean as she wished she would make her daughters wash the floor again, changing the water again and again and again, then gathering it with a rag to be squeezed all over again.

"It was awful," my mother sighed; then right away she would laugh. "But that's how we all wash the floor to this very day."

When she said "all" she meant not only her sister and herself but her sisters-in-law in Nahalal as well, Uncle Menahem's wife, Penina, and Uncle Yair's wife, Tzilla, who were expected to clean their mother-in-law's house as part of the qualifying and suitability auditions for entry into the family. They tell the same tale themselves, that they, too, continued with Grandma Tonia's cleaning methods for many years hence. There are habits that form in a person or a nation during times of slavery that are not broken even after the departure from slavery into freedom.

As for cleaning the walls, I mentioned earlier that Grandma Tonia had the walls of the kitchen and dining room and the hallways covered in oil paint halfway up so that they, too, could be washed. Here as well she had precise cleaning instructions, which everyone knows to quote: "First with wet, then soap, again with wet, finish with dry." I remember these words easily because her daughters and daughters-in-law recited them for many years, enraged and laughing, threatening one another with her traditional warning: "I'll take chunks out of you!" And they argued: Was it just with soap, or was it with a mixture of water and kerosene as well?

Several years passed and my mother completed her studies at the village school. In those days most village boys and girls studied only through the tenth grade, but especially gifted students—and those whose parents were interested—continued to the eleventh and twelfth grades in the Hanna Meisels Agricultural School at the entrance to Nahalal.

My mother was a very good student, but her older brother, Micha, had already gone off to Haganah courses and Menahem and Batsheva were still children and Yair was a baby. A sixteen-year-old girl was a source of labor that could not be given up easily. The house and the farm needed tending; there were cleaning and milking to do, eggs to collect, vegetables to pick, and feed to be given to the cows. Only many years hence did I understand why my mother read a certain poem for children, written by Kadya Molodovsky, the Jewish Polish poet, to my sister and me over and over again. It was the story of a little girl named Ayelet with a sky-blue parasol who had to draw buckets of water and hang shirts and socks, and there were knots to tie and buttons to sew and potatoes to peel and floors to wash . . . so it was in a far-off corner of Warsaw: marshland, a yard, a sagging house; and so it was here, too, in Nahalal: mud, a yard, and a spotless house.

Indeed, in spite of her will and her talents, my mother was not sent to complete her high school studies. Her friend Penina Gary, who did continue, told me how Batya would wait for her by her house when she came home from school, to ask what they had learned that day. Still, two years later, she went to the seminary in Jerusalem. There were many other moshav youth who did not finish the last two years of school, and these young people were sent by the movement to the seminary, which lasted several weeks, to broaden and deepen their education. There, in Jerusalem, she met my father, and the two were married about a year later.

8

Like the stories of the arrival of the sweeper from America, and like tales of the wondrous family jennet known as Ah, the wisest, most spirited, most *mutzlach* donkey in the Jezreel Valley and perhaps the entire world, about whom I shall tell later, and like the never-ending debates that took place—who worked hardest and who suffered the most and what was the size of the orchard behind the coop and who said this and not that to whom and where exactly did the black fig tree stand, and where the white one—there are several versions and shades of meaning to the story told about the meeting between my mother and father. These, however, are not all that different from one another, and they all attest to the fact that Grandma Tonia's cleaning issues were not confined to the narrow world of buckets, rags, prohibitions, and brushes. They affected the entire family, including my parents and even the love between them.

That meeting took place in 1946 when my mother came to that moshav movement seminary in Jerusalem. She was eighteen years old.

In Jerusalem she spent time with a young man from Kfar Yehezkel who was also attending the seminary. One day toward the end of spring they were walking down Jaffa Street toward Zion Square when it began to rain, a late and sudden downpour. As my father told it in his precise and biblical Hebrew, "the windows of heaven were opened," as if this were the Flood itself. My mother and her friend, dressed in light overcoats, went in search of shelter. The young man said, "My cousin lives not far from here; let's run to his place."

37

That cousin was my father, Yitzhak Shalev, a young teacher and poet just starting out, several of his poems having recently been published in the newspaper. He was twenty-six at the time and living in the center of town in a rented apartment in the home of the cellist Thelma Yellin. When his cousin from Kfar Yehezkel and an unfamiliar girl from Nahalal came bursting into his quarters with the spring storm, they took him by surprise and shook him up.

The guest removed her soaking overcoat, then freed her long, thick braid, which was dripping raindrops, and dried it on a towel he gave her. He served them tea, which she drank scalding hot and with great pleasure, her pinky finger extended alongside the glass. She had inherited this love of scalding-hot tea from her father and the finger extended alongside the glass from her mother, but my father gave no thought to such trifling matters. He gazed at her, and although he was not a religious man he decided that God had caused that rain to fall just for him.

Years later, long after they had married, he wrote a lovely poem about that meeting, called "Suppose." I reprint it here in its entirety:

Suppose you met a different man,
Suppose I found me someone else,
All would be different, my daughter not so fair,
Or maybe full of grace.
She would not weep when watching movies,
She would not cry at songs of woe,
And if she did she would not spread her
Flimsy hanky and mewl quite so.

Suppose the man was quite another
To whose smoking pipe you would agree

Even if he smoked much like I do
He'd never stuff his pipe like me.
All would be different, and so would you
Sad or happy you'd stride beside him
Down city streets instead of alleys
Racing after a man pursued by wind.
Other books would line these bookshelves
For you to shelve and air them out
Other guests would grace your presence
Other words would leave your mouth.

Suppose I found myself a different woman,
With darker skin, or lighter still,
Who casts a spell of thinning silence
Rendering my mad tongue still.
All would be different were it not for
A day of blusters and freezing clouds,
When you took refuge in my warm quarters
Your mantle of dripping hair a shroud.
Suppose that brimming cloudburst
Had simply not been allowed . . .

This poem still brings a smile to my lips and a tear to my
eye. The drafts were conversations he held with my sister and
me when we were small children. He would tell us again and
again the story of this first meeting of theirs, and he always
ended with that same fateful question that he later included in
the poem: "And so, children, what would have happened if that
downpour had not occurred?" Confused and frightened, we said
nothing, and so he would answer himself: "Mother and I would
not have met and you would not have been born!"

And while we were still digesting this terrifying possibility
he would propose another scenario that would make our heads

spin: "Or you would have been born, but to different people, and then you wouldn't have been you!"

But that downpour did happen and the meeting did take place, and my mother and father began to see each other even without the vicissitudes of weather. It did not take long before he brought her to visit his mother, Grandma Zippora, at the Number 2 Workers' Housing Units in Jerusalem, where she also met his younger brother, Mordechai, who was then eighteen years old. I note this because after that meeting my mother sent a letter to her sister, Batsheva, in which she mentions her new suitor for the first time. Among other things, she wrote, "I met two brothers in Jerusalem. Both are very smart and very ugly." Not long ago, when I told my uncle Mordechai about this letter, he burst out laughing. His wife, Rika, begged to differ: "That's not true," she said. "Yitzhak wasn't ugly at all."

Ugly or not, when my mother returned to Nahalal my father sent her letters to which she responded. At the time she had several suitors in the Jezreel Valley, all of whom were tall and sturdy, light-haired and blue-eyed—"Or vice versa," my father would say with the amiability of the victor—but more and more letters passed between Jerusalem and Nahalal, and where writing was concerned my father had no peer among the Jezreel Valley suitors.

As I have already mentioned, my father was, at the time, a teacher, and when the summer holiday began he wrote that he intended to visit relatives in Ein Harod, Ginosar, and Kfar Yehezkel, and asked if he might also visit her at Nahalal. When he appeared, seared by the sun, his skin red and flaking, she discovered that he had made long portions of the trip on foot in order to tan and strengthen himself so that he would not appear before her family in the shameful guise of the bespectacled, white, city-dwelling tiligent that he was.

Although he had wanted to make a good first impression,

my father arrived at a most inopportune time, which attested to his unfamiliarity with the lifestyle of the family he would one day be joining: he came during the Great Friday Morning Cleaning! And this lack of knowledge led to another mistake: he did not circle the house and enter through the back door, but knocked at the front and walked in before Grandma Tonia could shout "Around back! Come in the second door!"

When he arrived, my mother and Batsheva were airing the bedclothes between the platform and the laundry house. Grandma Tonia was worried that he would disrupt their work and so she glowered at him and instructed him to sit down, out of the way, while her daughters continued to air, beat, and wash.

The guest asked to help in some way, so Grandpa Aharon sent him out behind the chicken coop to sow cucumbers. It was out there that he erred for the third time. Grandpa Aharon told him to leave thirty centimeters between each cucumber, which he did, equipped with a ruler, pegs, and string. Another, more derisive, version has it that he used a level and a slide rule, while an even more stringent version claims that he also made use of a compass and a sextant because he wanted to show how good he was at measuring and planting properly. The spaces between the cucumbers were indeed extremely precise and the rows as straight as arrows, but after two hours the visitor had managed to plant only ten cucumbers.

This event earned my father the nickname *Sha*lev, with the accent mockingly on the first syllable and, as was customary in Nahalal, it was never forgotten. Many years later, even after my father had made a name for himself in other matters no less important than cucumber planting, the story was recounted at every opportunity.

As for the visit itself, everyone first believed that my mother had invited him because he was a poet and she was very interested in literature. But after dinner, when the two went out for a stroll in the fields, it became clear that Shalev was courting her with gusto and that she was interested in his company. Not much time passed before she left the village and followed him to Jerusalem—"Far, far away, to an unknown land" as in the Kadya Molodovsky poem—but issues of Grandma Tonia's cleaning even played an important role in my parent's wedding. This is how it was: When the two decided to marry, Grandma Zippora came from Jerusalem to Nahalal to discuss the necessary details with Grandma Tonia. The house and the yard were the natural and most suitable place to hold the wedding, but it was winter and Grandma Tonia wanted to postpone the ceremony until summer because, as she put it, "the guests will fill the house with mud!"

Shalev would not consent, either because he did not wish to wait or because he was already familiar enough with his future mother-in-law to suspect that in the summer she would ask to postpone the wedding because the guests would fill the house with dust. With regard to cleanliness, Grandma Zippora was far more lenient and relaxed, so the wedding was conducted instead in her Jerusalem apartment, which the guests from the Jezreel Valley filled with mud. After the wedding my parents rented a room in the home of Professor Roth on Abarbanel Street and thus, officially anyway, my mother became Jerusalemite, though she never lost her pride at being a daughter of Nahalal—pride that on occasion turned into arrogance, and the feeling that her origins granted her a uniqueness and distinction in her new surroundings. She felt this way her entire life, even when she had lived much longer in the city than she had on the moshav, and something of this she passed on to me—for better or worse.

She did it in the stories she told, in the comments she made, in the blushes she blushed, and in the things she chose to mock.

In particular I recall my first day of school, first grade at the elementary school in Kiryat Moshe, the neighborhood of Jerusalem where we lived at the time. As can be expected, this was a day of great excitement. She helped me organize my satchel, made sure I was washed and dressed properly, and took great care in tying my shoes, since every time I tried doing it myself I laced the laces through the wrong holes and got myself all tangled up.

I was sitting on a chair in the kitchen and she was kneeling in front of me, tying my laces into a double butterfly bow, perfectly symmetrical and lovely to behold, when, pleased with my general appearance, she took my hands in her own and said two important things: first, that I should not remove my shoes in school and walk around barefoot as she and I were in the habit of doing, because "these city folk" do not look favorably upon such things; and second, she said—as she rose to her feet and looked down at me, her voice enriched with a note of importance—"Every pupil will surely be asked who he is and where he comes from. And what will you say?"

"That I'm from here, from the Kiryat Moshe housing project, building number four."

"No!" she said. "You will tell them, 'I am the son of farmers from Nahalal!'"

Today, as I write these words, I grin to myself. Imagine a boy from the French or English or Polish countryside making such a statement on his first day of school in the big city. He would be a laughingstock! But the Israel of the 1950s was a different place, and my mother made it very clear what she expected of me: "That's what you'll tell them. 'I am the son of farmers from Nahalal!' Remember. Don't ever forget."

Many years later, sometime after the deaths of my parents—my mother passed away in the summer of 1991 and my father about a year later—I once again saw that uniqueness from a different angle, in a chance meeting with the author David Shahar, who had been a friend of theirs, one pleasant morning on Chopin Street in Jerusalem.

I was very happy to see him. I loved his books and recalled his visits with my parents, and when I was a young man I had the privilege of meeting with him privately at the home of Grandma Zippora at the Number 2 Workers' Housing Units in Jerusalem. Grandma Zippora was already dead by then; my father and his brother Mordechai had asked me to take care of something in her apartment. They told me that perhaps I would find David Shahar writing there, with their permission, and they warned me not to bother him with questions or interrupt his work.

But David Shahar had risen from the desk and initiated a conversation with me, and so I dared to ask him a few questions, the kind a young and enthralled reader asks a great and beloved writer. Among other things I asked him how he wrote, to which he replied with a question of his own: Did I write, or was I planning to in the future? I told him the truth, that on occasion I wrote a poem for the drawer, or for a girl, but I had no intention of becoming a writer. Rather, I was planning to be a zoologist, though I had not yet decided whether in the field of entomology, the study of insects, or ethology, the study of animal behavior.

He smiled and said, "If that's the case, then I'll answer your question. I write and perfect one page each day and I never, ever go back to it."

And now I, too, smile to myself, since today, when I am occupied with neither entomology nor ethology and I no longer write poems, either for drawers or girls, I think about him and his answer from time to time; unlike David Shahar, I am unable to write one perfect page per day and I am obliged to return again and again to my writing, to change and fix, to inspect in the light until the work has been done "good good" and it is truly clear and clean.

But back to our chance meeting on Chopin Street on a pleasant morning during that awful year in which both my parents died. I was walking toward the center of town and David Shahar was taking a morning stroll, elegant as usual, attracting attention with his intelligent features and his refined appearance. He wore a large black beret tilted foppishly over one ear, a colorful silk scarf knotted around his neck, and a long black overcoat draped over his shoulders and flowing downward like a cape. In one hand he was either leaning on or toying with a thin walking stick.

We greeted each other and stopped to speak briefly in the plaza outside the Jerusalem Theater. Quite naturally, the conversation turned to my parents. He scolded me for having started to write at a time he considered to be so late in life, and told me it was good that my parents had lived long enough to read my first novel, *The Blue Mountain.* Saddened, I told him I had also read to them—she in her sickbed, he in his—chapters from my second novel, *Esau,* as I was writing it, and how sorry I was that they did not get to read it bound and published. He told me that they were both very happy that I was writing and that my mother was particularly pleased that my first book had a connection to the Jezreel Valley and her village.

"She never relinquished her identity as a daughter of the Nahalal moshav," he said, affirming what I already knew. And then he added another statement, which I will not forget to my dying day, a sentence that could only be crafted by a writer like him, a writer capable of producing one perfect page per day, a page that needs no revision: "I remember the day your father brought her from the valley to Jerusalem," he said. "She was like a large red flower atop the stones of this sad town."

9

By the time my mother was pregnant with me, the War of Independence had erupted. In a besieged Jerusalem, there was not enough food or medical equipment or medications, and water was being rationed in tiny quantities. She preferred to give birth in Nahalal, and years later she told me another fine story: when she was in the eighth month of her pregnancy, her older brother, Micha, who was fighting with the Palmach Harel Brigade, put her in his jeep and smuggled her out of Jerusalem behind enemy lines by way of the secret Burma Road late one night.

She told me that he brought her to the town of Rehovot, and from there she tottered on her own until she reached my father's sister, who was then living in Tel Aviv. "She didn't even offer me a cup of tea," my mother recounted, reddening. From Tel Aviv she continued by herself to Nahalal.

My mother never blushed from embarrassment, only from anger, and the way she blushed was unique—a deep reddening that did not bloom on her face but rose from her chest to her brow like berry juice poured into a glass. Grandma Tonia, too, would blush with fury, but with her it was focused in her left cheek, which reddened more than the right.

My mother often emphasized the veracity of a story with the family decree—"This is how it was"—but many years later, after her death, Uncle Micha himself provided a different version. He called my mother's recounting "very nice" but incorrect. He said, "This is not how it was," and confirmed that my mother was in her eighth month of pregnancy and had indeed left Jerusalem for Nahalal, but that there had been no daring night escape in his jeep; rather, she had departed in an organized caravan that was evacuating children and the infirm and the aged and pregnant women from Jerusalem to the coastal plain.

My father joined her in Nahalal close to the birth, but we left some two weeks later in the wake of a huge row. Grandma Tonia had announced to my mother that her maternity leave had ended, using one of her most cutting expressions—"Stop stinking up the bed!"—as a way of informing her that she had spent enough time being pampered and that she must get up and clean and cook and work; that in her Ukrainian village of Rokitno the peasant women gave birth in the field, tied their newborns to their breasts with a kerchief, and continued to reap the harvest and gather the sheaves.

My father bellowed with rage and vetoed Grandma Tonia's plan. He made it clear that his wife deserved more rest, and certainly a respite from such hard labor. In spite of his educated pronunciation, his eyeglasses, and his white skin, Shalev was assertive and quick to anger, while Grandma Tonia was unrestrained and more experienced than he in family quarrels. Now both had stirred, provoking one of the best imbroglios in our family's history. To my chagrin, I was only two weeks old and remember nothing of it. But I have been told that voices were raised and insults hurled, that my father grew even paler than his usual city pallor, and that Grandma Tonia's left cheek flared red.

And then Shalev struck his mother-in-law with the shrewdest arrow of them all: he said that he could not stand her because she reminded him of his own mother!

For a brief moment she was stunned. This poet, who had failed at so simple a task as planting cucumbers, had suddenly proved himself more wily and dangerous than foreseen. In no time she was fuming mad, because she could not stand his mother either, and because she was angry with herself—how could she have failed to think of this first? After all, she could have preempted him and told him he reminded her of his mother. And anyway, how can one react to such an insult? Had he said that Grandma Zippora was better than she, she would already have known how to respond. But what could be said to someone who denigrated his mother-in-law for being too much like his own mother?

But Grandma Tonia would never be rendered speechless. She got hold of herself at once and dredged up a particularly nasty slur, which no one had ever heard of before or understood, but which, too, has become part of our family dictionary of expressions and which we use to this very day. She turned to my mother, who all the while had not said a word out of bewilderment and discomfort, and said to her, "You watch out, Batyaleh, this guy is one decent bird!"

What exactly did that mean, "One decent bird"? No one knew; even today, the meaning of this expression is unclear to us. It could be that Grandma Tonia made it up at that very moment, possibly translating from Yiddish—"*a yenner foigel*"—or Russian. My uncle Yair once came up with another explanation. He said that "one decent bird" could be referring to Grandma Zippora's name, which means "bird" in Hebrew. In other words, "for out of the serpent's root shall come forth a viper": Shalev was like his mother; the apple had not fallen far from the tree.

No matter what she really meant, it was clear to everyone who heard it that this was not something good. Indeed, when my father heard this one decent bird swoop from the mouth of his mother-in-law he stood up, enraged, and packed a suitcase. And because he would not and could not return to besieged Jerusalem with a newborn baby and a woman who had just given birth, we three traveled to Tiberias.

I do not recall that journey either, of course, but I was told we stayed for a few days in a hotel. My father had a cousin living nearby at the time on Kibbutz Ginosar, and she helped him find work there. He began teaching in the kibbutz elementary school and my mother became a nanny in the communal baby house.

We stayed at Ginosar for four years, and my very first memories come from there. We lived on the shores of the Sea of Galilee in a lean-to with walls of hanging cloth and fruit crates for storage and a roof made of palm fronds. I remember a strong easterly wind blowing against the flaps and causing them to billow, and I remember joyfully bathing with all the other children from the baby house in a large cement bathtub. And one other image: I am sitting on a wooden plank, floating and rocking in the lake. The plank is a mere five feet from the shore and my parents are standing next to me but my heart is filled with terror.

I remember, too, visits by Uncle Itamar. Itamar and my mother were very close, despite the fact that they were born to two different mothers and despite his bad relations with Grandma Tonia. At the time he was an officer in the army and was stationed at the Northern Command headquarters nearby. Each time he visited, he and my mother would drink scalding tea and imitate their father, Grandpa Aharon, who always complained that the boiling tea he was given was "as cold as ice," and they vied to recall quotes from books they loved and spent a lot of time laughing.

Another uniformed soldier would visit us as well, diminutive and dark—my young aunt Batsheva, who was serving in the Nahal Fighting Pioneer Youth unit. She came to tell and grouse to my mother that Grandma Tonia was angry: Shalev had taken her Batyaleh and the Israel Defense Forces had taken her Shevaleh, and now she was left without her cleaning crew. She had combined pressure and pleading and had managed to convince whoever it was that needed convincing that the family farm was doomed if Batsheva was not granted an early discharge. But then something unexpected happened: Batsheva rebelled; she signed a waiver and continued to serve in the army. Her mother and father were furious with her beyond reason. She told me that in their extreme anger they very nearly came to blows with her, but it did not help; she preferred to stay in the army. She said that it was pleasant and interesting for her, and I allow myself to imagine that no master sergeant in the IDF could ever have been as stringent about cleaning as was her own mother.

10

Many years before that, in 1928 or 1929, an incident occurred that can be seen as a starting point, a seed sown that caused everything else to happen.

This is how it was: On a winter day when battalions of clouds stormed over the Carmel mountain range from the west and covered its crest, and the eye of heaven turned dark and rain was falling outside and the fields of the valley became muddy pools, Grandpa Aharon received a letter from his older brother Yeshayahu, the double traitor.

He opened the envelope and got angry. First of all, the letter was written in Yiddish, the language of the Diaspora, the language that he himself had thrown aside from the day he arrived in the Land of Israel. But what raised his ire even more was the contents. Uncle Yeshayahu wrote that he had heard about the difficult economic conditions in Palestine, specifically those in the Jewish farming communities, and thus he was sending American dollars, for he wished to aid his brother the pioneer.

The rain did not let up. Marshy sludge filled the yards and

the cows and the farmers waded knee-deep in it, hearts filled with winter cold and woe; there were no coats or boots for the children, wallets were empty, and along came this cheeky letter from his rich brother who, instead of settling the Land of Israel, had started a business in Los Angeles.

Conditions at the time in Nahalal were abysmal. The work was hard labor, the income infinitesimal, the mud not only the reality of winter but also a successful representation of all the other seasons of the year. Many families, including ours, came to know true deprivation and distress; some left, but still Grandpa Aharon was unhappy with his brother's generous gift. On the contrary, he was insulted to the very core of his being. American dollars?! He, who had come to the Land of Israel and drained the swamps, who had plowed the first furrows in the homeland, who had planted and sown, would not touch such capitalistic money from the Jewish Diaspora. Moreover, he was no beggar and was in no need of handouts from rich men, even if this rich man was his own brother.

Grandma Tonia, practical as ever, pleaded with him, saying that they needed the money for winter coats and boots and for kerosene for the Primus stove and the lantern and for sugar and oil and flour and medicines. But Grandpa Aharon was stubborn and insistent, and he did something wrenchingly difficult: he sent back the tainted money to its sender, along with a few choice ideological rebukes. According to another version, Grandpa Aharon added a few personal insults as well, along the lines of We, the pioneers who are causing the wilderness of our homeland to blossom in a Zionist and Socialist manner will not fall prey to temptation in the form of money earned by exploiting the proletariat by traitors who chose life in the Diaspora and changed their name from Yeshayahu to Sam.

In spite of the many differences between the two brothers, they were similar in temperament; thus, Uncle Yeshayahu also grew angry and stubbornly insistent and sent back other envelopes, with more dollar bills in them, which caused Grandpa Aharon to do the same thing he had done the first time without even bothering to read his brother's solicitous words of temptation. The mere sight of the depraved glow of the greenbacks through the envelope was enough to make him send it back to Los Angeles, unopened just as it had been sent to Palestine.

In the end, Uncle Yeshayahu was also offended—like Grandpa Aharon, to the core of his being. From the time he had emigrated to America he felt his younger brother was critical and arrogant and convinced of his own superiority. Now that he had returned his letters and his charity and had even made unpleasant comments about him, he too was so hurt that he decided to retaliate, to take revenge—nothing cruel or violent, heaven forfend, but rather an elegant and intelligent and educational revenge, the revenge of a firstborn and practical son against his young, idealistic brother. My mother told me that he thought it out carefully, made a scheming plan, and, primarily, waited for the best moment. He was a practical man, and he was patient.

Two or three years passed, the envelopes from America no longer arrived, and Grandpa Aharon calmed down. But the situation did not improve. In 1931 the poverty and privation were so bad that he went in search of work, which he found with the Workers' Council of Binyamina, and the family moved there from Nahalal for a year. Micha and Batya were then seven and four years old and Grandma Tonia was pregnant with the twins, Batsheva and Menahem. Uncle Yaacov, her younger brother, did his best to keep the farm running at Nahalal with the help of the two older brothers, Moshe and Yitzhak, who were living in nearby Kfar Yehoshua.

As I have already said, Grandpa Aharon had neither the

inclination nor the strength necessary to withstand the difficulties and shoulder the burdens and the pressures of farming. He was, however, a master planter who knew how to get rid of harmful pests and was expert at pruning and grafting, and he had true affection for the symbolism of farming. The first plantings on his farm were grapevines and olive trees, pomegranates and figs, since these were among the seven species of the Land of Israel according to the Bible. His cypress trees were arranged at the entrance to the property just as they were around King Solomon's bed. But best of all were the citrus trees he planted by the house. I recall one in particular, his special citrus tree that amazed me and piqued my curiosity since it bore several types of fruit that he had grafted onto the base of a single bitter orange tree.

There are a number of family versions with regard to the varieties of citrus growing there. The arguments always began with "He grafted oranges, lemons, and grapefruit onto the bitter orange tree," then passed on to specifics—"Shamouti oranges, Valencia oranges, pomelos"—and ended with "This is where Grandpa's special citrus tree stood, which bore pears, plums, and pineapples." Today I understand that there was nothing truly of note in this, that any citrus grower could graft several types of citrus onto a single base. But at the time I thought my grandfather was a wizard, and I gazed at him and at his miraculous tree in disbelief and wonder.

As I have already recounted, every once in a while Grandpa Aharon would announce that he had a headache and then take off, though sometimes he simply disappeared without explanation and Grandma Tonia would say, "He's runoff again," and she would set out to find him and bring him home. If he ran away to his sister, Aunt Sarah, in Herzliya, then the pursuit was relatively simple. If he found shelter at Kibbutz Hanita, where his sons Itamar and—for a while—Binya were members, then the pursuit was impossible, since Grandma Tonia would not set foot there. Sometimes he ran off to Rehovot, to his friend Ze'ev Smilansky; their friendship has been recorded for posterity in the book *Preliminaries* by Smilansky's son, the writer S. Yizhar. And sometimes to Tel Aviv, to his friend Haim Shorer, who had been his neighbor in Nahalal until he left to become the editor of the workers' newspaper *Davar*.

My grandfather also responded with great enthusiasm to David Ben-Gurion's request that farmers from the older moshavim provide guidance to new communities founded by recent immigrants. For several months he taught the Hasidic residents of Kfar Chabad—who were at the time considering the possibility of engaging in productive agricultural labor—to graft and to prune grapevines and fruit trees. He himself was secular, having abandoned religion on principle, but he was well acquainted with and liked the songs the Hasidic men sang—he had learned them at home as a child—and he sang them with gusto. Several are etched quite precisely into my memory, especially "My Soul Thirsts for You," thanks to its beauty and sweetness, as well as another because of the special way he would enunciate the words, taken from the book of Numbers:

And on the Sabbath dayayayay
Two lambs of the first year without blemish
And on the Sabbath dayayayay
Two lambs of the first year without blemish
Ay yay ya ya yay
Ya ya ya ya ya ya ya ya yay
Ya ya ya ya ya ya ay yay ya ya ya ya yay . . .
And two tenth measures of flour for a meal offering, mingled with oil
Mingled with oil
And its dri-hi-hi-hi-hi-hi-hink offering
And two tenth measures of flour for a meal offering, mingled with oil

54

Mingled with oil
And its dri-hi-hi-hi-hi-hi-hink offering

The penultimate word of the song appears in its shortened form in the passage from the Bible—"drink"—but this is the way Grandpa sang it, as did the Hasidic men who came to visit, and thus I must record it.

For years after he finished instructing them, two men from Kfar Chabad would come to visit before every Passover holiday, year after year. Their beards and sidelocks looked just like those in the photos of Grandpa's father, and they seemed so out of place to me in the human vista of Nahalal. They would always bring the same holiday gift—a bottle of schnapps and *matza shmura,* the special unleavened bread they baked themselves for the holiday.

Grandpa Aharon enjoyed the attention they paid him and the conversation and the singing and the schnapps, but nothing more than that. As mentioned, he was not exacting in observing Jewish law; in fact, if there was anything exacting about his observance it was in his nonobservance of the law. Incidentally, he was none too impressed with the Hasidic, or Jewish, custom of waving one's pedigree around, bragging about some forefather who was an important rabbi, and this aversion he passed on to his descendants. When someone would boast to my mother about some Jewish scholar or leader or rabbi in the family, she would respond drily: "We're not just plain folk either; we're descended from the Golem of Prague."

As for the special Passover matza itself, it indeed graced our Seder table, but in our house bread was consumed during the holiday as well, the bread Grandma Tonia baked in the wood-burning, mud-and-tin Arab taboon oven that Binya built near the wall of the cowshed when he was a boy. Once a week Grandpa Aharon would use a large bowl to knead the dough that Grandma Tonia would then shape into loaves. While the loaves rose she would start a fire in the oven, get it roaring good and hot, and bake them—during Passover as well—into wonderful bread.

"On Seder night we eat matza and do everything we're supposed to," she would explain, "but during the rest of the week we need to work, and without bread there is no strength for working." Indeed, we held the Seder according to tradition: we read the entire Hagaddah and sang all the songs and drank all the requisite glasses of wine. The only problem was with the *afikomen* that Grandpa hid for us children to find; he never bought the gift promised to the child who found this special piece of matza.

Two *afikomens* are remembered to this day in the family. One was during Passover of 1963, which we celebrated at Aunt Batsheva's home in Kfar Monash. Grandpa Aharon hid it so well that neither the children, nor the adults enlisted to help them, ever found it. In spite of all the pleas and requests and promises, he returned to Nahalal victorious, without ever revealing its whereabouts.

The other *afikomen*—I don't recall the year—was never found either, for a different reason. Grandma Tonia picked something up in order to give it a swipe with her shoulder rag—dirt can be found even during the Seder—and she discovered a piece of matza lying there, which she popped into her mouth without giving it a thought and without knowing that this in fact was the *afikomen* that Grandpa had hidden. That was the official explanation, though there are cousins who claim this was one of the few instances in which the two actually cooperated—that she ate the *afikomen* with his knowledge and encouragement.

In addition to giving instruction to communities planting orchards, Grandpa Aharon had other jobs and occupations. Every one of them served him as a city of refuge, and several even brought in a few extra coins for deposit in the empty family purse: he was in charge of keeping track of annual rainfall in the Nahalal area, he was the registrar for the identity cards issued by the Interior Ministry in Tiberias and the Jordan Valley, and he was responsible for the village eucalyptus grove. In those days, every self-respecting moshav had a eucalyptus grove from which the farmers chopped branches to be used as posts for building pens and fences. Unlike pine or cypress trees, for example, the eucalyptus grows new branches in the place where the old ones have been lobbed off, and it was Grandpa Aharon who determined which eucalyptus trees in the Nahalal grove could be used so that there would always be more branches for those who would need them in the future.

With regard to keeping track of the rainfall, each winter my grandfather appointed himself to monitor several rain gauges, which he visited regularly in order to take measurements and record them. He published the results in the village bulletin. In general he was interested in the weather and possessed extensive knowledge about it beyond the usual for a farmer, who quite naturally must know about rain and hail and frost and drought. He was good at predicting the weather as well, and he told beautiful stories about winter clouds and how he could guess the amount of rain that would fall by the way they gathered atop the Carmel mountain range.

With regard to the identity cards, the citizens of the newborn state were asked to return their British Mandate documents in exchange for new Israeli identity certificates. Grandpa Aharon received a locked trunk filled with blank certificates, forms, and rubber stamps. He passed from village to village and the residents would line up before him with their Mandatory certificates and other identifying documents. He met friends—some of whom, according to Grandma Tonia, were female—he chatted, shared memories, and filled in the new identity papers in his beautiful penmanship, then signed and stamped them with the seal of the Interior Ministry.

Grandpa Aharon produced and signed the first identity cards held by my parents, who were then living at Ginosar. But when Grandma Tonia learned that a hotel room had been set aside for his work in Tiberias, she rushed there before "his whoors" could arrive. Grandpa Aharon was a handsome man with a sense of humor who knew how to tell a story, and Grandma Tonia gave the nickname "his whoors" to all those women who were chasing after him, either in reality or in her imagination.

Once, Grandpa Aharon even made a "runoff" as far away as the desert, to the "phasphatte" plant by the Dead Sea (this was how Grandma Tonia pronounced it, and we have never been able to bring ourselves to call phosphates anything but "phasphattes"). Just as he did in our yard in Nahalal, he had begun to gather and arrange parts and sacks and ropes and metal pipes so that very quickly he had become a sort of keeper of the commissary. Imagine his surprise when, several days later, a busload of laborers arrived at the plant carrying not only the laborers but one small figure floating toward him in the shimmering heat—Grandma Tonia, who had located him and followed him all the way there, and who would soon go to work in the plant kitchen.

As I recount all this my heart breaks. Grandpa Aharon was no great and *mutzlach* and industrious farmer and was not suited to a backbreaking life in agriculture, as it was then, but he was very creative and talented in ways that the *mutzlach* and industrious farmers of his generation were not. I have asked myself more than once—and I ask it now as well—what would have become of him had he traveled to the United States like his brother did. Apart from the fact that a different woman would have ducked into my father's rented room in the rain and my siblings and I would not have been born, he might have had a better life: he might not have lost his first wife, Shoshanna, or been forced to measure rainfall or "runoff" to the desert, or be in charge of eucalyptus trees, or fill in and distribute identity cards. He could have spoken and written in Yiddish and published stories and articles in *Forverts* instead of *The Young Laborer.* And who knows? Instead of funny songs for the Passover Seders he led at Nahalal, perhaps my grandfather would have written musical comedies for Broadway and become a rich man and enjoyed "luxuries" without pangs of guilt, and maybe, like Uncle Yeshayahu, he would have changed his name from Aharon to, say, Harry, and would not have thought of his brother as a traitor and this brother would not have plotted how to take revenge on him and how to help him and how to win his heart back and he would not have sent him dollars in envelopes or a sweeper in a large wooden crate covered in stamps and addresses.

II

After four years at Kibbutz Ginosar my parents returned to Jerusalem. At first we lived in the Nahalat Shivah neighborhood in a cold, damp room I do not remember at all, and after a year we moved to the apartment in which most of my childhood and youth took place—a recently built block of apartments in a Kiryat Moshe housing project. That is where my sister Rafaela was born and, much later, our brother Zur, who is nineteen and a half years younger than I. It is he who begat Roni and Naomi, who painted my toenails with shiny red nail polish in the first chapter.

The apartment block in Kiryat Moshe did not have the Jerusalem ambience that the neighborhoods my father and David Shahar wrote about in their books did. Certainly not the ambience of Nahla'ot, Beit Yisrael, Street of the Prophets, the Kerem neighborhood, Bak'a, the German Colony, or any of the other old stone areas of the city. There were no stone archways, no alleys of geranium and jasmine, no domes or vaulted ceilings, and the ugly tenement blocks of Kiryat Moshe had never heard of the Jerusalem regulation about being built of stone. They were built of brick and covered with gray stucco.

Nearby, however, there stood like sentries three very Jerusalem institutions: the Jewish Institute for the Blind, the Ezrat Nashim madhouse, and the Diskin Orphanage. These institutions had a very strong presence in our lives. Many of the madhouse residents were in the habit of wandering around the neighborhood and were a permanent and interesting part of the local scene. Terrible shrieks of misery would rise on occasion from the Diskin Orphanage, spanning the distance to our ears and filling our hearts with horror. We had a special connection with the children from the Institute for the Blind. Sometimes we played with them—even games like tag and hide-and-seek—and sometimes they told us stories and we told them stories, and sometimes, on hot summer nights, the whole lot of us, blind kids and sighted kids together, peeped through the windows of the blind girls' bedrooms. We watched the girls as they prepared for bed while the blind boys pinched our arms and whispered with great excitement: "What do you see? Tell us what you see . . ." They were far more inflamed than we. The eyes of their imaginations saw scenes that our flesh-and-blood eyes did not.

Years later, in one of my conversations with my father about his beloved city, I told him that for me Jerusalem is not the Temple Mount, not the Mount of Olives, not the roof of the Notre Dame monastery, not the markets or the neighborhoods or the alleys that he described in his poems and stories, but the madness and blindness and orphanhood of those three institutions. And he, to my surprise, smiled and said that I was far more correct than I could have imagined.

There, in that block of apartments, my mother had a small garden into which she poured all her knowledge and all her longing for the Jezreel Valley and for the earth and farming. She would toil there barefoot, in a work shirt and short pants that caused even the blind passersby to swoon. A little farther up from her garden, where the Mercaz Harav yeshiva now stands, was a rocky open field where the cowherds of nearby Givat Shaul would pasture their cows. Although they were Jerusalem cows, they were like a wave and hello from Nahalal. She would spy them from the kitchen window and fill with joy. "There's a nice heifer out there. I'm going to have a little chat with her," she would say, and off she went, trumpeting shrilly as a shepherd would, her fist pressed to her lips like a small horn. She did not "return back" empty-handed, either; she would bring back cow droppings with which to fertilize her garden.

In spite of the fact that a number of years had already passed since she had left the village and her parents' home and had a family and a home of her own in Jerusalem, and there was no one to force her to clean, no one to pull her out of class or threaten to take chunks out of her, she washed the floor exactly as her mother did: she did not use a squeegee; instead, she bent at the waist and, moving backward, passed a rag over the floor in a long, wide, zigzagging motion, proud of her flexibility, her ability to touch her feet with ease.

And when she wrung the rag into the bucket she checked the water pooled there in the light, then smiled apologetically and said, "I'm afraid I've caught a bit of her malady." Everyone knew which malady and whose it was. Even after Grandma Tonia died, and up to the day of her own death, if someone in the family showed excessive interest in cleanliness, my mother would call him or her Tonia, even if it was she herself.

Since my mother taught me to sew buttons and iron shirts and patch trousers and cook a meal and other tasks that in my day were taught only to girls, one day I also got a floor-washing lesson from her.

A few minutes into the job I noticed that she was watching me wring the rag with an amused look on her face. She asked whether I thought I had squeezed all the water out. "Sure," I said. "Every last drop."

She took the wrung-out rag from me and squeezed it so that more and more water flowed forth.

I was surprised. And maybe even a little hurt. She told me what her mother had told her when she was a girl: that men wring with strength and women wring with intelligence. Men hold the rag with both palms facing down so that they twist only their strong hand while the other holds the rag in place, "providing contrast," as the professionals say. But women—all the more so if they are women from our family, which is to say graduates of the Floor-washing Department of the Grandma Tonia University of Cleaning—do it like this: one palm faces upward while the other faces down and both hands do the wringing, moving and turning until the arms cross and straighten so that an additional torque of twisting and another ninety degrees of turning and squeezing have been achieved.

On occasion my mother's sister or brothers would pay us a call. In particular I remember the visits of Uncle Menahem, since before such a visit my mother would prepare a list of things that needed fixing in our home. My father was not familiar with and did not wish to become familiar with any labor beyond that of changing a lightbulb, and I must admit that I inherited that trait from him. My mother's brothers, on the other hand—as with most moshav men in those days—knew how to fix and build and pour cement and tile a floor and connect waterpipes and electrical cables. And when, as a child, I read the children's poem "I have an uncle in Nahalal / and he can do it all" I was certain it had been written about them.

Uncle Menahem always brought a few tools with him when he came, since he knew he would not find them in our house. They had wonderful names like *jabka* (vise grip), *izmil* (chisel), "the little Swede" (adjustable wrench), and the "personal pliers that every moshavnik needs," and when he laid them out on the table my father grew anxious, lest these repairs that his young brother-in-law was about to carry out threaten his male status in his own home. At once he would pace in circles around Uncle Menahem, and when Menahem changed the gasket on a dripping faucet or wound linen fibers around screws or unclogged a drain, my father gave him instructions.

One such event I remember clearly. This is how it was: Uncle Menahem, in short pants and tall work boots, stood on a chair atop the kitchen table, screws and nails in his mouth and tools poking out of his pockets and hanging from his belt. He connected wires, changed a light socket, and hung a new lampshade from the ceiling. My mother held the chair legs in place, I watched my uncle with admiring eyes, and my father moved around the table telling him, "Not like that . . . tighten it a little more . . . take that off first and then screw in that part . . ."

Uncle Menahem looked down at him from atop the chair, at first with astonishment, then with impatience, until finally he spat out the screws and nails into his hand and said, "Shalev"—accent on the first syllable, of course—"Shalev, do me a favor, go write a poem . . ."

There were a number of facets to the Nahalal-Jerusalem tension in our family, some amusing and others less so. The famed circular street plan of Nahalal was no less important to my mother than all the holy places of Jerusalem; she missed her family and the village even though she had left them. Shalev, on the other hand, found Grandma Tonia to be unbearable, pitied Grandpa Aharon, and sensed that though my mother's siblings accepted him into the family, they did not do so with pleasure. They criticized his right-wing opinions and made fun of his two left hands—criticism that he returned in kind, and quite cleverly, on his rare visits to Nahalal, when he would go down to the turkey shed and shout, "Long live Socialism!" As turkeys do, the foolish fowls responded in an excited chorus of agreement, which would cause Shalev to smile broadly and say to all those present, "You see? That's how it's done. It's quite easy . . ."

Thus, since my father tended not to visit Nahalal very often, and my mother, who wished to strengthen the connection between her children and her family and home, could not travel because my sister was too small, I was sent several times on my own in the village milk truck that came frequently to Jerusalem.

I was five years of age when my mother first decided I was old enough for such a trip. She awakened me at two-thirty in the morning and we first of all drank tea—hers, scalding hot, mine, poured into a saucer so it would cool quickly because "It's already time to go to Tnuva! Motke the driver and our tanker can't be kept waiting."

"Motke" was Motke Habinsky and "our tanker" was the Nahalal milk tanker, a Mack diesel that brought Nahalal milk to the Tnuva dairy. At the time, the Tnuva dairy was in the Geula neighborhood of Jerusalem, a forty-five-minute walk from our apartment—the walk of a young mother, one hand holding the hand of her sleepy child, the other carrying a small suitcase.

It was dark and chilly outside as we walked down to Herzl Boulevard past the Mekasher bus company garage. From there we turned left, ascending toward Romema and passing by the Allenby monument and the Aboud-Levy stonecutters' courtyard, where, on our way to the market, I would hear the song of the chisels being played, but which at this hour was silent. It was as if the air had been rent just where the singing should have been.

We passed the Camp Schneller military base and continued along the Kings of Israel Street, the main thoroughfare of Geula. Here and there the first synagogue-goers scurried by, but not a single car passed us or could be seen from afar. Years later, when I was around twenty, I had a strange and pleasant experience connected to that nighttime walk: nearly every night for a period of some three weeks I dreamed that I was walking, alone, down that same street, from Camp Schneller to Sabbath Square, occasionally stomping on the pavement and kicking off from the ground in a high, slow skip lasting some five hundred feet, and at the high point, the top of the arc, I soared above all the buildings, finally landing gently, only to repeat the whole process again. Aeronautical dreams are not rare, but why was it precisely there that I flew, and why so many times in a row? I do not know. After twenty nights of dreams those nightly flights ceased, and I am very sorry about that.

At that time, however, my mother and I were walking on the ground. We reached Sabbath Square and turned left and left again at the dairy. Our tanker, a semitrailer emblazoned with the sacred name of Nahalal in bold yellow lettering on its green doors, was already parked there, a thick pipe sucking the milk from it. Motke Habinsky bellowed, "Hello, Batyaleh!" addressing my mother as everyone in the village called her.

Motke was a boisterous, warmhearted man with thick and hairless arms and legs and a large face that beamed with good-heartedness. He shouted like all truck drivers did—"because you have to be louder than the engine" he told me years later, when he was old and I came to ask him questions—and he looked just like a Jewish truck driver from the Jezreel Valley should: thick-set and beefy, in a blue work shirt; wide, blue short pants; and *sandalim tanakhi'im,* the biblical sandals that everyone wore at the time.

This was during the Period of Austerity in the early fifties, and Motke pulled out a package from underneath his seat that had been prepared by Grandpa Aharon and Grandma Tonia for their daughter who was wasting away in exile in an afflicted city, and which contained a plucked and headless chicken, several eggs, a block of cheese, some fruit and vegetables of the season, and two letters of complaint, one from him about her and one from her about him. It was all wrapped in brown wrapping paper that Grandpa Aharon had cut from an empty sack of milk powder and padded with old newspapers and bound with a piece of straw pulled taut and tied tightly, like two crosses.

Grandpa Aharon was very good at packing and tying, which appears to be a family trait; each time my mother told me the story of the vacuum cleaner that Uncle Yeshayahu sent to Grandma Tonia from America, she noted that he had packed and padded and tied it all up properly in preparation for its prolonged and punishing journey, in "just the way that Grandpa Aharon packed the packages he sent us from Nahalal." The two were brothers-in-packing who knew how to pad and bundle and wrap and tie and did not trust another soul to do it for them.

"Who do you belong to?" Motke shouted at me, even though he knew the answer.

I was too flustered to answer. Motke took hold of me and tossed me—practically hurled me—into the heights of the driver's cabin and told my mother to climb in after me. For a moment I thought she was coming with us and I didn't know whether to be happy or sorry, but she informed me that she would only be going as far as the entrance to the city, near our neighborhood.

Motke backed up our tanker with ease—at that time I did

not know just how hard a feat that was—and pulled out of the Tnuva lot and into the street. He turned right and began upshifting the gears as we drove up Kings of Israel Street.

"How are things in the village?" my mother asked.

"Just fine. Lots of hard work."

"And at my house?"

"Your house? What's the matter, don't they write to you?"

"Yes, but not enough."

Sitting between the two of them, I was concentrating on Motke's hands as they busied themselves with the steering wheel and the gears. I cast a wistful gaze at the short cable that hung above his door—the cable to the Mack's horn.

Motke took in my gaze. "Seems to me that someone here wants to toot the horn," he said.

I did not answer for fear of ruining my chances.

"Would that be you, Batyaleh?"

My mother could easily have said yes and done it herself. But she declined. "No," she said, "toots and horns don't interest me in the least."

"So maybe it's me?" Motke asked himself, then answered, "No, couldn't be. I toot the horn enough."

After a long and frightening silence he said, "So who's left?" And he turned to me. "Only you. You want to toot the horn a little?"

"Yes."

"So what are you waiting for? Stand behind me and pull," he said as he leaned forward toward the steering wheel. I squeezed into the space between the seat and his broad back and tugged on the cable. A loud lowing resounded in the air, filling me with both terror and joy each time.

"Harder," Motke said. "Let's wake up all the religious idlers and city folk. Enough sleeping, you bums; get up and work. We have a country to build!"

I tugged the cable again, harder this time, and the Mack horn boomed and trumpeted a challenge to the shofars of Jerusalem of every generation, and to the ultra-Orthodox who, every Sabbath, demonstrated against the Tnuva trucks that brought farm produce to the city on that holy day, and who ran for their lives when kibbutznikim and moshavnikim brought into the fray attacked them with the wooden handles of hoes in order to beat a path to the vegetables, eggs, and milk thay had worked so hard to bring to market.

I returned to my place and watched Motke's hands turning and pressing and shifting and pulling, and his sandaled feet as they danced on the three pedals, the one at the right, the gas pedal, made of wood.

Motke stopped at the entrance to the city. My mother gave me a kiss and climbed down from the heights of the cabin. "Wave good-bye," Motke told me.

She waved and I waved back, but I turned my gaze to Motke, excited about the drive ahead.

"Now get some sleep," Motke told me. "The road is long and when we get to the village you'll be expected to help out. The calves'll need water and the chickens will need to be fed and alfalfa has to be brought to the cows and Grandma Tonia will be wanting you to help clean. Sleep so you don't get there all tired out."

Now, as I write of these matters, I think of my mother returning to our flat in that block of apartments, to my father and my little sister, who was half a year old at the time, and I try to imagine what was on her mind as she walked. Then, however, I gave it no consideration. We left the city, cruising downward toward the coolness of the bend in the road at Motza, then up the Castel with winding difficulty. I was captivated by the freedom and independence, by the nighttime hilly journey and by

Motke's expertise behind the wheel of the enormous tanker as it rose and fell and twisted with the road, and by the proximity to Motke himself, who was in my eyes the epitome of manhood. And so I traveled, without knowing where we were or in which direction we were headed or what the time was, slipping from sleep to wakefulness and back again. Till this very day I remember those trips to Nahalal as a series of identical dreams, since from time to time I would awaken, and each time the air would be warmer and the light brighter. En route, Motke stopped in a big city—apparently Tel Aviv—and had me climb out of the semitrailer to stretch my bones like he did and to pee together with him behind the back wheels. This is how he let me know he considered me an equal: me, a little boy from the city without a driving permit for a semitrailer, but the son of Nahalal farmers and a real man.

After that he took me for a breakfast of omelet, yogurt, and salad, and even ordered a cup of coffee for me. "Drink up, it's all right," he said. "And don't tell your parents I let you." From there we went to hand over a few packages and letters and pick up others from a large building, probably the headquarters of the Israeli Labor Movement, and then back to our tanker, which was waiting patiently in the street.

The country, smaller then than today, was large and spacious, and our tanker, smaller than today's semitrailers, was much larger than they. When we reached the end of the Wadi Milkh road, which everyone called Wadi Milek, near Yokne'am, and the Jezreel Valley suddenly opened up and spread out before us, I felt as though we had come out on the other side—the good side—of the world. A dozen years later, when my parents learned to drive and bought a car—a little Simca 1000—which my mother used to drive to Nahalal, this was the very place at which she would take a deep breath and smile to herself without saying a word, maybe even without noticing the depth of her breath or the broadness of her smile or the almost sigh she sighed.

Motke parked in the center of the village, by the wall of the dairy. He told me he had to "take care of the Mack" and make some notes in the auto log—words that made a deep impression on me—and that I should wait for Uncle Menahem, who would soon be coming to the dairy and would take me to Grandma Tonia.

"What if he's already been to the dairy today?" I asked.

"He hasn't. Your uncle is always the last to arrive. Don't you know that?"

While waiting for Uncle Menahem I watched the goings-on at the dairy in hopes that one of the farmers would activate the separator. The separator was a machine of magic, a round container with a handle at the side. When the handle was turned, the container spun with great speed and the milk poured inside it separated into cream and skim milk, which traveled down two different tubes to two different jugs. That morning, however, no one was separating cream from skim milk, so I sat watching the farmers as they arrived at the dairy with their wagons and horses and milk jugs, talking vociferously among themselves and regarding me with a look familiar to every child in the village.

The people of Nahalal in those days had a very special sense for evaluating children, and also an ability to appraise and predict, which probably derived from all those years of observing calves and foals. This enabled them to foretell the future of each newborn—at home or in the barn. They knew who would be a good farmer and who would be a loiterer. Who would be a *mutz-lach* and contribute and be useful, and who would be a parasite, exploiting the principle of mutual aid and becoming a burden on society.

The farmers who recognized me asked after my mother;

those who did not asked whom I belonged to. That is how things were back then—every child was asked to whom he belonged. When the inquirer got his answer, everything became clear. The child could be placed on the map of stories, events, people, rumors, successes, failures, and, mainly, in the cattle pedigree logs of the village, the movement, and the local and familial gene pools. These matters were so sharp, meaningful, and precise that even back then I understood it was better for me to say I was the son of the admired, beloved Batyaleh than to say I was the grandson of Grandma Tonia, who was different, estranged, and controversial.

Motke was right. As always, Uncle Menahem was last to arrive. The dairy manager was already showing signs of impatience and glared at me, as if I were responsible for his tardiness. I even felt a certain guilt, since that was what I had been taught: family means responsibility and mutual aid. But then something white appeared from afar—our horse, Whitey—pulling a wagon with a few milk jugs on it, along with the dark image of Uncle Menahem himself, sitting on the wagon, holding the reins and idly smoking a Noblesse cigarette.

Uncle Menahem was full of mischief. He had been smoking since the third grade and started riding motorcycles two years later. He chased cats, mimicked people, told stories, and made a lot of people in the village laugh or get angry. At about that time he married Aunt Penina, the most beautiful girl in Nahalal, and it was at their wedding that I did something terrible that was not forgotten many years hence.

As mentioned, this was the Period of Austerity, and in preparation for the festivities Grandpa Aharon had collected eggs to be able to present to all his favorites: my mother; Uncle Micha and Aunt Batsheva, who no longer lived at home; and a few other special guests. He placed the eggs in a small basket that he hid in the cowshed and which I found, together with another boy, a "relation of no blood."

Whitey stood nearby eating his modest equine repast as we—and here I wish to remind your honor that we were four and a half or five years old—we hurled an egg at him. The deep yellow of the yolk on his white coat impressed us greatly and encouraged us to continue, so when Grandpa Aharon summoned the guests to the cowshed to receive their bounty—ten eggs apiece—the horse stood in front of them dripping profusely. "All we needed were bread crumbs and we could have made delicious schnitzel for everyone," my mother would add every time someone spoke ill of her son.

Some of the relatives—in my opinion, they too were relations of no blood—hastened to spread the story through the entire circular street that was Nahalal. Incidentally, no one was surprised, just as they were not surprised years later when I showed up at the inauguration of the old Haganah arms cache with toenails painted a bright, shiny red. That is what happens when a child carries in his chromosomes the genes of a citified, Revisionist father, a tilignat, and those of a grandmother who cleans all day long, closes off rooms, and imprisons vacuum cleaners behind locked doors.

12

Uncle Menahem patted me roughly on the head and said, "Hey there. What's up?" as if it were absolutely natural that his sister's young son from Jerusalem would be waiting for him at eight-thirty in the morning at the Nahalal dairy. He removed the jugs from his wagon and poured the milk through the white cloth diaper that covered the weighing pans of the scale, all the while arguing about something with the dairy manager, just as he was always arguing about something with someone. When he finished his business he seated me on the wagon, placed my suitcase next to me, handed me Whitey's reins, lit a fresh Noblesse cigarette, and said, "Go."

Handing me the reins was more than just a game. It expressed an approach that is disappearing from the world, one that gave small children a feeling of worth, the feeling that they are being trusted and given responsibility and, later, that they are expected to contribute and make themselves useful.

Excited and nervous, I said "*Dee-yo!*" to Whitey—which is "giddyup" for Hebrew-speaking horses—the first time hesitantly, the second with confidence, and the third with authority. He backed up the wagon, made a sluggish turn, and began the carefully measured walk home, prolonging as much as possible this pleasant gap between the morning chores that had been completed and the hard labor that awaited him later in the day.

Whitey was a handsome horse, a bit theatrical, one that should have been pulling a carriage through the streets of Tel Aviv or even on the Champs-Élysées or in Central Park, but instead he found himself sunk in the mud of the Jezreel Valley up to his eyeballs. He was not as strong or diligent as other horses in the village—real workhorses—either physically or mentally. But he had inspiration and a sense of humor, and he loved to perform. Sometimes, when Uncle Menahem or Uncle Yair said something funny—which happened often—it seemed as though Whitey smiled, too.

More than once, Whitey got away, usually for the purpose of paying nighttime visits to mares that enraged other farmers because they resulted in foals who did not see hard work as their main purpose in life. Nonetheless, my uncles refused to geld him as the other farmers had done to their workhorses.

Menahem and Whitey

They said that gelding was a terrible thing and that farm animals suffer enough as it is.

Uncle Menahem was also enjoying a legitimate moment of repose. He sat on the wagon smoking with pleasure and asked me about his sister. But I was focused on the path and the reins, pulling left and right and saying *"Dee-yo!"* again and again. I was fully aware that Whitey knew the way home and was politely ignoring me. He descended from the center of the village to its circumference; when he reached the circular road he turned left, then after passing the Yehudai, Shalvi, Yannai, and Tamir farms turned right into our yard, the Ben-Barak farm.

The wagon proceeded down the lane of tall aromatic cypresses at the entrance to the farm—trees planted by Grandpa Aharon and since then uprooted—and stopped by the old hut. This is where the jugs were washed and where one could spot the first sign of Grandma Tonia: the cheese that she rendered dripping from the cloth diaper where it hung.

I jumped down from the wagon, walked to the door of the porch, and, because already then I knew it was forbidden to enter, called to her from outside. I could hear her standard response of excitement from inside the house: "Oy, how good that you're here . . ." When it was my mother who had arrived she was greeted with "Oy, how good that you're here, maybe you could just . . ." followed by a request. But I was still young and devoid of any real usefulness. She came outside, bent down to me, and gave me happy, loving hugs and kisses free of her usual claims and complaints.

Now the ritual ceremony could begin: Grandma Tonia took hold of my chin with one hand, leaned away from me while at the same time scrutinizing me, and said, in her Russian-Yiddish accent, "You look vorn down." Then she seated me on the low wall of the porch, which was as wide and as low as a bench and was good for sitting and even lying down, and said, "*Ah-nu,* sit down a minute. Wait here for me, outside."

She went into the kitchen and I could hear the refrigerator door opening and closing. At our house in Jerusalem we still had no refrigerator, only an icebox, but Grandma Tonia already owned a refrigerator, and not just any refrigerator but a Frigidaire, which she had also received from Uncle Yeshayahu.

She returned from the kitchen with a spoon in one hand and a jar of cream in the other. "*Ah-nu,* open your mouth," she said, dipping her spoon into the jar and raising it, white and dripping, near my mouth. A drop of that cream is not a drop like any other; first, it hangs on a short, thick string, and then the string lengthens and becomes a thread and the drop thickens and grows larger until it plunges to its target—a slice of bread, a cup of coffee, an extended tongue.

On its first day, when it came to life in the separator, the cream was runny. Only later did it grow firmer until it finally became butter. Usually it would be spread on bread with Grandma Tonia's plum jam, but I preferred it with salt and a thin slice of tomato and, best of all, if there was any, a piece of "herring tail," Grandpa Aharon's favorite. I would eat it with tremendous enjoyment, and my grandmother would watch me and exclaim, "That's heredity for you," which is what she always said when one of the children looked or behaved like one of the adults in the family.

I opened my mouth wide and she dribbled the contents of the spoon inside. "*Ah-nu,* swallow."

The cream trickled onto my tongue toward my throat, leaving an unbelievable, shameless taste behind that surprised me each time anew. I swallowed. She squinted at me and proclaimed, "You already look much better."

And although I knew I was in the midst of a very funny moment I did not laugh. Everything seemed too true and important for me to laugh, and even today I am certain she was right. I must have looked "vorn down" a moment earlier but already looked far better by then.

"Are you hungry?" she asked. "Go wash hands. I'll make a meal for you."

Without thinking, I turned toward the door of the house, but Grandma Tonia rebuked me. "Hand-washing in the trough! Outside!"

The trough—a low cement sink large enough for three small children to stand inside easily—stood at the corner of the paved pathway near the house. That was where buckets of water were filled for washing the floors and where the hose was affixed for rinsing the pathways. Dishes, hands, feet, and faces were washed there, and if it was a child being cleaned off, then the trough became a full-body shower.

I washed my hands, ate, and Grandma Tonia asked me what

time I had woken up in order to catch my ride. I told her with pride that I had risen at two-thirty in the morning, to which she replied, "I'll prepare your *mishkav* and you can take a nap." That's the way she always said it: she never used the usual word for "bed," always *mishkav*.

I loved that word. Back then I still thought it was something Grandma Tonia had made up, but with time I discovered it in the Bible, from which my father would read whole chapters to us nightly. I knew the word meant "bed," as in "David arose from his bed," but although my father never explained anything he read to us, I felt there was something else hidden within, something far more rousing than just sleep, as the way the word was used several verses on: David "took her; and she came in to him, and he *lay* with her . . ."

Some dozen years later, when we were learning the medieval Jewish poetry of Spain in high school, I recalled Grandma Tonia and the literary influence she had had on me as I studied this lovely poem by Abraham Ibn Ezra:

When I come to the patron's house early in the morning, they say:
"He has already ridden away."
When I come in the evening, they say: "He has already lain down to
sleep."
He either climbs into his carriage or mishkav—*woe to the poor man,*
born to misfortune!

This made me very happy, a feeling that did not usually characterize my reaction to high school literature classes in general, and medieval Jewish poetry in particular. But I took great pleasure from the fact that the history of the Hebrew language linked the linguistic purity of Ibn Ezra and the Bible to Grandma Tonia's unique style, which was at the same time rich and inarticulate.

And so it was that from the *mishkav* of the king of Jerusalem and the *mishkav* of the patron of Spain I came to my humble *mishkav* in Nahalal, which my grandmother prepared for me in her Levite chambers, the small room adjacent to the Temple—the two locked rooms—and the Holy of Holies, the bathroom where the sweeper, Grandmother's vacuum cleaner from America, resided in isolation.

Many times I asked permission to enter that room in order to see it, with its brushes, its various heads, its large wheels, its thick tube, and its shiny canister, all of which my mother had described to me. But she refused. Perhaps she was afraid I would ask to have it; the truth is, Grandma Tonia was not particularly generous and refused all sorts of other requests. She even had a set phrase she would employ each time someone asked for something she had in the house but did not use: "You're not going to inherit me as long as I'm alive!"

In that matter I have special recollections of a large beer stein that made me curious as a child and covetous as a young man. It was big and heavy and made of glass, and the word MÜNCHEN was engraved on the bottom. No one in the house or the family drank beer back then, and when I asked my grandmother where she had gotten the beer stein, she said only that it "came from the Germans" without explaining any further. I would imagine that she meant it was taken from the nearby German colonies, Waldheim and Bethlehem of Galilee, after the English deported their residents during World War II. When I asked my grandmother for the mug her response was the usual: "You're not going to inherit me as long as I'm alive!"

"So just open the door for me," I suggested now, "so I can have a look at the sweeper from outside, without going in."

"Absolutely, positively, no!"

Imagine, then, my utter astonishment when, quite recently, while conducting research to write about her and about her sweeper, I learned that my cousin Nadav, the oldest son of Aunt Batsheva and Uncle Arik, had managed to persuade her to let him enter the locked bathroom. And not only that, he even bathed there!

It happened many years ago, when Nadav was about seventeen years old. He had no interest in the sweeper and had not asked to see it; it is unlikely he had steeped himself in matters of the sweeper as I had myself. But he had made a bet with his mother that Grandma Tonia would let him bathe in her tub, where no person in our generation had ever bathed. He made his wager and won. He took a real bath there, one that lasted a full hour!

How did he manage it? No one knows. "It was simple. I just convinced her," he told me with a sly and patronizing smile when I asked him to explain.

I felt hurt and envious. Nadav is five years younger than I, and it was clear to me that such privileges were reserved first and foremost for me, the eldest grandson, and not the dozens of less significant grandchildren that followed. I consoled myself with the possibility that this was not an intentional slight on the part of my grandmother, but something trivial and ordinary, like Grandma Tonia asking Nadav to fix something in her house for which he demanded as his wage the chance to bathe.

Unlike me, having inherited my father's two left hands and two shortsighted eyes, Nadav has the able hands and sharp eyes of his father and uncles and knows how to fix and build and assemble everything inside and outside the house, as well as tractors and cars. Did Grandma decide to pay him back with a bath in her forbidden tub? She cannot answer because she is dead and he will not affirm or deny it, and when I sat with him and tried to get to the bottom of the secret of his success he smiled that same infuriating smile and said, "I convinced her," as if he were saying, "and you didn't manage to."

"What do you mean, you convinced her?" I wondered aloud. "Did you promise her something?"

"No. Nothing."

"Did you threaten her?"

Nadav was horrified. "Threaten Grandma Tonia? You don't know me, and apparently you didn't know her, either."

"You probably told her you'd made a bet with your mother and you offered to share your winnings with her."

"No," Nadav said, "I convinced her. She was a logical person, not like you think. And you know what? That's the reason I took a real bath there while you write fiction about that same bath."

"And did you see the sweeper?" I asked, ignoring this latest provocation.

"The what?"

"The sweeper. Her vacuum cleaner."

"I didn't see anything special," he told me.

"What's with you? How could you not have seen it? A giant, American, General Electric vacuum cleaner as big as a barrel, made with a sparkling canister, black rubber wheels, and a tube at least two inches in diameter. Hasn't your mother ever told you about it?"

"She's mentioned it. She even asked her for it."

And indeed, the two of them, his mother and mine, asked for their mother's sweeper a number of times. "Why should it go to waste in your bathroom," they said. "Give it to one of us." But Grandma Tonia had refused them, too, with her usual motto: "You're not going to inherit me as long as I'm alive!"

"So you didn't see it there?"

"There were all kinds of packages and boxes, but I didn't see anything as big as what you're describing. You put too much faith in your mother's stories."

When I understood that Nadav was enjoying this conversation far more than I was, I abandoned the campaign.

Getting back to the *mishkav* my grandmother made for me, the bed—despite the regal solemnity of its consonants and vowels—was nothing more than an old iron cot wider than a single bed and narrower than a double, upon whose springs and strips of metal had been placed three small seaweed-filled mattresses all in a row.

In that very room and on that very bed I was destined to sleep many times. One of them, about seventeen years later, was with an American girl by the name of Abigail, whose contribution to the story of my grandmother's vacuum cleaner is priceless. But now, at age five, I slept there alone. And since by then I already knew how to read and write, before falling asleep I perused back issues of the children's supplement of the *Davar* newspaper, which were kept in that room in an old bookcase, from the time when my mother and her siblings were small.

Unlike my parents, Grandma Tonia allowed me to read as I pleased without imposing a lights-out time. But wake-up time was a different matter altogether. It was always very early and in the same manner: at five-thirty in the morning she would enter the room, and without uttering a word she would grab hold of the middle mattress of the three and pull it out from underneath my body in one swift motion. While still asleep I would slam against the bedsprings and strips of metal, each time surprised, stunned anew. And Grandma Tonia would say, "*Nu,* I see you're already awake, so please get up. I need to start cleaning." If I did not hasten to do as she asked she would say, "Up, up, enough stinking up the bed."

I would get up, wash my face in the trough outside, and in the meantime Grandma Tonia would already have appeared in my room with a bucket and a rag, the windows and shutters wide open and the daily floor-washing under way. She would wash and squeeze and pour and check in the light again and again until the water was completely clear and clean and she was satisfied. She wrung the rag intelligently, like women do, and hung it to dry on Grandpa's special citrus tree.

13

In the annals of the Land of Israel, 1936 is known as the year in which the Arabs began to rebel against the British, but several other important things happened in that year as well, and these helped Uncle Yeshayahu carry out his revenge. I have already written about one of them: that year in Nahalal, proper homes were built to replace huts and tents. The village and its buildings were connected to the electrical grid—news that was published in an American Jewish newspaper read by Uncle Yeshayahu. Incidentally, Grandma Tonia took advantage of the opportunity and cooked meals for the electric company workers as a way of adding a few pennies to the family budget.

The second thing was that rumors of her cleaning mania had spread all the way from the Jezreel Valley in Palestine to Los Angeles, California, in the United States of America—not by way of the Jewish press but in the way that rumors spread. This is how it was, my mother told me: first the rumors traveled the circuit of Nahalal; then, as if from an irrigation ditch, they leaked out to the fields. So that I would understand more clearly she opened the Brawer atlas to the "Map of the Lower Galilee and the Valleys" and, with a yellow pencil, showed me the perimeter of the Jezreel Valley. Here is Nahalal, here is the

Carmel range, here is the Kishon River and Mount Gilboa and Givat Hamoreh. The rumors rose up from here and flowed until the entire valley was submerged.

There lived in the valley at that time many friends of her father, pioneers of the Second and Third Aliyah—in Ein Harod and Kfar Yehezkel and Kfar Yehoshua and Merhavia and Tel Adashim—and the rumors soon reached the peaks of the Carmel, from which they quite easily poured westward to the Mediterranean, at which point my mother shut the Brawer atlas and placed the small globe I had received for my birthday on the table, since from here on the rumors spread throughout the entire world.

But how? Quite simply, as rumors spread: they took wing and floated into the air. At first they flew above the Mediterranean Sea over Crete and Sicily—here, these islands right here—and from there by word of mouth and from island to island until they reached the Straits of Gibraltar, which I found rather surprising; not that these rumors existed at all but that the stories my mother told me about her mother and the stories my father told me about Scylla and Charybdis, about Icarus and Odysseus, were told with the aid of the very same globe and took place in the very same locations.

The rumors crossed the Atlantic Ocean and reached the shores of America. They soared over the Appalachian Mountains and the Great Plains, over the mountains and the deserts of the Wild West, until the point of the pencil came to rest on California. So sharp was that pencil point that it poked right inside Uncle Yeshayahu's office window in Los Angeles, here, right at this spot.

"And then what happened?"

Indeed, this is how it was: Just then, Uncle Yeshayahu was reading the article in the newspaper about the new buildings that had been erected in the village and how they were connected to the electrical grid. He added this printed news to the rumors flying about, then closed his eyes and smiled to himself. All at once, everything was clear. Grandma Tonia's cleaning habits, the new house, the electrical grid—these were all one in the same. The issue of his revenge had found a perfect solution: Uncle Yeshayahu decided to send his pioneering brother and his pioneering sister-in-law a vacuum cleaner! An electric vacuum cleaner, large and heavy, one that his brother could never ever hope to return as he had returned the dollars in the envelopes.

As befits the revenge of a double traitor, this was a double revenge, since Grandpa Aharon would be unable to return this gift for two reasons: first, because he did not have the means to send such a large and heavy package, and second, because Grandma Tonia would never agree. She would want this vacuum cleaner for her cleaning.

" 'There are many devices in a man's heart, but the counsel of the Lord, that shall stand,' " my mother intoned. She was not a religious woman but she knew her Bible and was enchanted by the mocking tone of this verse. She quoted it with great pleasure because in this instance she knew what was to come; even Uncle Yeshayahu, a sly and seasoned businessman, could not have guessed what would happen—that even if his present was not sent back in scorn it would be imprisoned in a locked bathroom and left unused, and not even by his brother but by his brother's wife, the person for whom the gift was intended. But why? The answer to that I shall reveal anon.

Uncle Yeshayahu rose to his feet, told his secretary to cancel all his afternoon appointments, donned his top hat—that's what American capitalists and members of the Tel Aviv bourgeoisie wore in those days, not the burlap sacks folded into hats, or "dunce caps," worn by pioneers—and set out for a large appliance store owned by a fellow Makarovite, a man from the city from which he and my grandfather hailed. Uncle Yeshayahu approached the store owner and said, "*Gib mir dem groiser, dem schwerer, dem schtarkster un dem bester shtoib-zoiger was du hast!*"

I could not believe my ears. Yiddish? From my mother's mouth? As I have already mentioned, her father stopped speaking Yiddish the moment he arrived in the Land of Israel. "Yiddish is the language of exile!" he proclaimed, and, to my consternation, it was cut off from his descendants. So how did my mother declaim this sentence so fluently? I only found out years later that in order to be able to tell this story she had approached Moshe the butcher, who had a small butcher shop next to the grocery in our neighborhood in Jerusalem, and asked him how to say in Yiddish "Give me the biggest, heaviest, strongest, and best vacuum cleaner you've got."

"Mrs. Shalev," said Moshe the butcher, astonished, "what do you need this Yiddish for? Are you buying a vacuum cleaner from the ultra-Orthodox in Meah She'arim?"

"No," my mother said.

"I told her it was a pity," Moshe the butcher himself informed me many years later, "because if it was a vacuum cleaner you wanted, Mrs. Shalev, well, my in-laws' neighbor happens to be selling one for a very good price, and with him you can speak Hebrew."

My mother said, "No, thank you. I am not buying a vacuum cleaner. I need the sentence for a story I'm telling my son."

"Very nice," he said, quite pleased as he wrote the sentence she requested on a slip of paper. "A woman from Nahalal, the daughter of pioneers, tells her *yingaleh* a story in Yiddish."

The Makarovite store owner showed several good, strong vacuum cleaners to Uncle Yeshayahu, but he said, "*Groiser! Groiser!*" and "*Schwerer! Schwerer!*" because they were not big enough or heavy enough for his purpose. The Makarovite asked if he wanted an industrial-strength vacuum cleaner for his furniture store, to which my uncle replied no, that the vacuum cleaner needed to be a home cleaner, but the biggest and heaviest and strongest.

In the end, Uncle Yeshayahu purchased a "svieeperrr" made by General Electric, which I imagine both he and the storeowner pronounced the same, with a *v* in place of the *w* and a long *ee* and a rattling Russian *r*.

Uncle Yeshayahu paid for the vacuum cleaner and asked that it be packed in a sturdy wooden crate suitable for one setting off on a long and difficult journey.

"Where are you sending it?" asked the store owner.

"To the Land of Israel!" Uncle Yeshayahu proclaimed ceremoniously.

"Jerusalem . . ." muttered the owner.

At this point in the story it becomes clear that Uncle Yeshayahu was a triple traitor. As if it were not enough that he was a capitalist living in America under the assumed name of Sam, now even Jerusalem was a trivial matter.

"Even this svieeperrr couldn't clean Jerusalem," he said drily. "I'm sending it to the Jezreel Valley. Maybe there are a few more swamps for my brother the pioneer to drain there."

14

On my grandfather Aharon's side I am the fifth grandchild, the first son of his first daughter, born to his second wife. I was preempted by Itamar's two sons and Binya's two daughters.

On Grandma Tonia's side I was the first grandchild. She took great pleasure in me, whether because I was the first or as an answer to the grandsons and granddaughters born to her husband. I, too, favored her—over my other grandmother, Zippora, and over Grandpa Aharon (my father's father, Meir, died before I was born), as well as over the way she was as described by a number of neighbors and relatives.

Instead of suffering from her claims and complaints, I enjoyed her love. She did not expect me to clean the house. She did not turn back the hands of the clock and cause me to arrive late to school so that I could beat the rugs or wash the walls, and she never threatened to take chunks out of me. The demands she made of me were few and sensible: that I not enter the house, that I not make things dirty for her, that I not scritch her walls, that I go to the cowshed and bring some "pigeons to lunch"— not, incidentally, for the purpose of dining with us—and that I should not go anywhere with empty hands; I was expected to take small packets of rubbish out to the cow's muck and "return back" with milk, eggs, and plums that had fallen from the tree and could be made into jam.

These are all undeniable facts, along with feelings and memories that cannot be changed. But beyond this I must repeat that in our family there are several versions of every event. Some can live pleasantly side by side with others, while some are so contrary that they cause quarrels. And although many of our family members are farmers, we are not always good at separating the wheat from the chaff, or the cream of stories from the skim milk of facts. There are members of our ranks who argue more about how many rows there were in our first vineyard than about who was the favorite child or who suffered most from Grandma Tonia or various love affairs. That is why I suspect this book will generate arguments and even an uproar among us—what is referred to in family parlance as "umbrage will be taken."

There is precedent: When my first novel, *The Blue Mountain*, was published, my uncles and aunts arranged a family party in its honor in Nahalal. I traveled there with my mother, the two of us happy and excited, but when we arrived we discovered that this "party" had certain aspects of a field court-martial. Several of our relatives had discovered bits and pieces of familiar stories and characters in my novel, and I was expected to defend and explain every paragraph in which I had not told the truth or, far worse, I had.

To my surprise, Uncle Menahem sat quietly smoking his umpteenth Noblesse and maintained a polite silence. It was only toward the end of the party that he stood up and announced that he, too, wished to make a comment.

"About what?" I asked apprehensively. Uncle Menahem could be very aggressive and forthright.

"About the donkey that could fly," he said.

Among the many characters in *The Blue Mountain*, I had written about a certain donkey named Katchka who made night flights from his stall in Palestine to Buckingham Palace in London, where he would converse with the king of England about the Jewish settlers in the Land of Israel and the future of Zionism. I had taken the idea from a story Uncle Menahem himself used to tell me when I was child, and which I loved, about the jennet they had before I was born, the one and only Ah—the wisest, most spirited, most *mutzlach* donkey in the Jezreel Valley and perhaps the entire universe. Everyone would recount tales, in tones of awe, about her intelligence and cunning, and Uncle Menahem would add that she was so clever that she knew how to open the door to the cowshed even when it was locked and bolted.

"This is how it was," he said. "She would pick the lock with a 'wire-piece' [Grandpa Aharon's word for a piece of metal wire], go out into the yard, look to the right"—Uncle Menahem tilted his head to the right—"look to the left"—Uncle Menahem tilted his head to the left, a slightly donkeyish look on his face—"and when she was certain no one was around, she spread her ears and flapped them like this and ran with great speed"—

The family with Ah

Uncle Menahem would flap his arms and run about the yard in a ridiculous gallop, imitating a donkey wishing to lift off into the air—"and she took off and flew."

"So what's your comment?" I asked. "What is the problem with the flying donkey in my book?"

"I'll tell you what the problem is," Uncle Menahem said gravely. "The problem is that the story isn't true!"

"I know that the story isn't true," I said, as the laughter died down. "Even back then, when I was five years old and you told me that story about Ah, I knew it wasn't true, that donkeys and jennets don't fly. But I liked the story and decided to use it in my book."

"You don't understand a thing!" he said, clearly angry. "You didn't then and you don't now. And that is why you made such a big mistake. Ah flew all right, but not to London to speak with

89

the king of England! She flew to Istanbul to speak with the Turkish sultan!"

"When Ah was born there was no longer a sultan in Istanbul," my mother interjected, further angering Uncle Menahem. He said, "What does that matter, anyway? Can't you see we're telling stories here?"

Uncle Menahem told lots of stories, some of them true and some of them made up, but he was a busy farmer who did not write and had little time for reading. Still, although it may not have been his intention, he gave me an important lesson in literature, which I have tried to adhere to ever since. In this book, too, which tells a true story about real people, he guides me, lighting the way. And thus it is that I have known the story of my grandma Tonia's sweeper for years according to my mother's version; when the family became aware that I was writing it, three additional versions were passed on to me at once, one of which I will tell hence, while the other two were made up—I have no doubt about it—on the spot, because they smelled an opportunity to be published. So, I shall stick to the version of my childhood, as told by my mother, which began with her father's arrival in the Land of Israel and his brother's immigration to the United States.

This was another occasion on which she used my little globe. Sometimes I wonder if they bought it for me to learn geography or so that she could use it for the purpose of telling family stories. She stood it on the table and spun it with one hand while the other held the yellow pencil and floated over the spinning globe, pointing out Russia, Europe, the Atlantic Ocean, and the United States.

"This is Ukraine, where they came from," she said. "This is the Black Sea. Grandpa Aharon walked from Makarov to Odessa—here, from this place to this one—with his Makarov friends, Sneh and Benyakov."

Benyakov was Ben-Yaacov, Yitzhak Ben-Yaacov from Kibbutz Degania, but my mother and her sister and brothers always imitated their parents when they told stories about them. Grandpa Aharon, Nahum Sneh, and Benyakov—they were known as the Makarovite Trio, she said proudly—made it to Odessa. From there they boarded a ship that sailed to Istanbul—here, there's the gateway to the Black Sea—and from Istanbul they sailed to Jaffa, here, in the Land of Israel.

"But my father's older brother, Uncle Yeshayahu"—by this time the pencil had already returned to Ukraine, where it traveled by train from a city called Kiev to the German port of Hamburg, and from there crossed the English Channel and the Atlantic Ocean—"went to America to do business."

At this point she grimaced. "Business" meant what bankers, salesmen, and peddlers did, which we had had more than enough of in the Diaspora; here in the Land of Israel we needed farmers and laborers, teachers and fighters and scholars. She had a loathing for "speculators"—those who traded in stocks and property—so strong that she forbade me from playing Monopoly, a game of property traders whose wives oppressed workers and crushed laborers and chewed chinga and had their hands manicured while the men bought and sold the people's lands upon which they built hotels for other speculators and capitalists, all of whom were waiting for prices to rise as they rented and invested and profited.

"Land is for planting and seeding and building and plowing and harvesting, not for buying and selling and making profits without working!" she proclaimed. It was only years later, when my sister was older, that she agreed to remove Monopoly from the list of banned games and, later still, even took part. To our dismay and her embarrassment, she turned out to be a first-rate speculator, competitive and lucky, whose business dealings spread across the board and whose coffers filled with money, while we, her children, spent most of our time bankrupt in the jail at the corner of the board.

But to return to that moment when Uncle Yeshayahu bought the sweeper from the Makarovite in Los Angeles: my mother, who, unlike me at the time, had actually seen the sweeper and could describe it precisely or, as is the case with tales told in our family, in a manner more precise than reality, said that Grandma Tonia's sweeper had "a large and shiny canister as big as a barrel."

It had "four large black rubber wheels" on which the sweeper moved from place to place.

It was "as big as a cow but quiet as a cat."

It had a suction tube that was "black and pliable, long and thick" and came with "lots of different heads" that could be affixed to the tube and could be counted on one's fingers:

A special head for cleaning floors.

A special head for cleaning carpets.

A special head for cleaning curtains.

A special head for cleaning sofas.

A special head for cleaning armchairs.

It also came with a special head for cleaning small drawers and a special head for cleaning large drawers, and some of the heads even had brushes, and since at that time I had never seen any kind of vacuum cleaner, I pictured the heads as real heads, with open, sucking mouths and dense, bristly hair.

As I have already recounted, not only Grandpa Aharon but also his older brother was good at wrapping packages. Thus it was that Uncle Yeshayahu wrapped the sweeper and its cardboard packaging in a soft, cloth sack, and placed it on a bed of rags and newspapers and sawdust inside a wooden crate that he fastened into place with straps and another layer of rags and newspapers and sawdust between the sweeper carton and the sides of the crate. After that he shut the lid of the crate and called a worker of his to nail strong, thin metal strips all the way around it.

When the worker had finished the job, Uncle Yeshayahu sent him to a hardware store to buy a can of black oil paint, a small brush, and tin templates of the letters *A, D, E, V, H, I, T, L, N, O, P, S,* and *U,* and when the worker returned he had him paint the crate with two inscriptions.

The first, which my mother wrote on a piece of paper, beneath the list of letters, was as follows:

SAVTA TONIA
NAHALAL
PALESTINE

The second was THIS SIDE UP so that the sweeper would not travel upside down and get a headache in all its heads at once and decide to run away.

The first time I heard this part of the story about the sweeper I was six or seven years old, and those thirteen letters were the first letters of the ABCs that I encountered. That was how the inscription written by Uncle Yeshayahu on the crate and my mother on the piece of paper became the Rosetta Stone from which I learned to read words in English.

With the help of the letters that formed the name of the village and my grandmother's name, as well as "Palestine"—the meaning of which my mother explained to me—I was able to complete and decipher the names of the cities etched on the glass panel of the stations on our old radio: SOFIA, BERLIN, PARIS, ROME, LONDON, ISTANBUL, and others, and because I knew all those names from my little globe as well, where they appeared in Hebrew, and because some of them were the flight destinations of Ah the jennet, I was able to master the other letters of the English alphabet.

As for the name and address of the addressee—SAVTA TONIA,

93

NAHALAL, PALESTINE, which is exactly how it appeared on the crate—the matter led me to entertain the possibility that even in America everyone knew her, just like in Nahalal and the Jezreel Valley. But my mother explained to me that there was a limit to her mother's reputation. The name of the country and the village were written on the crate, so once it reached Nahalal there was no longer a problem: in the village, everyone knew her, because she was one of a kind, my grandmother.

15

In general, when a literary hero sets out on a journey, the other characters take leave of him with sadness or joy at his departure, accompanying him to a train station or airport, or not accompanying him at all. That is true, too, for the readers and listeners of travel tales, who wish to learn not only the progression of the journey and its results, but also the reasons for which it was undertaken—even if those are not always explainable.

The journey my mother recounted to me, that of her mother's sweeper from Los Angeles to Nahalal, was quite different from the other travel tales that she and my father told me, different from the literary journeys I read about later—those of Jacob in the Bible, Lassie, Odysseus, Captains Hatteras and Ahab and Grant—because this was not a character in a book but a real one, and not a human being but a creature made of metal and plastic and rubber and cloth. But this took nothing away from the excitement of listening to the journey itself, or the need of the teller in telling it, or the soul she breathed into the story's hero, or the many details she inserted into the plot. For my mother had a method of her own in which she removed a rib from her family narrative and breathed life into it for the purpose of creating reality.

So, after Uncle Yeshayahu bought his gift for Grandma Tonia, and after he wrapped it properly, the sweeper was loaded onto a red truck—in America there are many trucks, and many of those are red, not just the green of our Mack diesel—and transported it to a large train station with dozens of platforms, not just one like our train station here.

At the train station the sweeper boarded a long freight train and traveled the length of an imaginary line drawn by the yellow pencil from west to east, the width of the entire continental United States. Nearby, in the carriage, were other packages and crates and boxes holding tools and merchandise and garments and appliances—maybe even other vacuum cleaners—but none of them was setting out on such a long and arduous journey, and certainly not one of revenge, simply one of cleaning.

Finally, at the big dock in New York—right here—the sweeper was loaded onto a large ship, and while it was dangling from the end of a rope on a crane, before descending to the dark below-deck depths, it could hear the shrieks of seagulls and the tooting horns of tugboats, and if it had not been sealed inside a crate it would have seen the Statue of Liberty and the skyscrapers and passengers in top hats and suits, and a steam-pressed and polished captain with four gleaming gold bars on the whiteness of his sleeve.

A departing horn blast sounded outside, along with the noise of pistons and engines and the rattling music of rolling-up chains and vibrations unfamiliar to the vacuum cleaner, whose whole being and very nature was that of smooth, horizontal movement, and here it was swinging to and fro, rising and falling on the waves. At first it was alarmed, then it calmed down slightly, and in the end it grew accustomed and even enjoyed itself. It listened to the pounding of dancers' feet in the ballroom, smelled the wide sea and the smoke from the tall chimney stacks, and when it heard the sounds of seagulls and tooting horns it knew it had once again reached a different port. This was Rotterdam, in Holland, on the opposite side of the Atlantic. The yellow pencil was right there with it, even though it had flown over the ocean faster than any ship or plane.

Here the sweeper parted from the polished captain with the gold bars and was tossed onto another large train, not as large as the American train that had brought him from Los Angeles to New York but large enough, much larger than the train we took from Jerusalem to Haifa.

This train brought him to the capital of France—yes, here, that's Paris, you see?—and France, you should know, is the land of *Fattypuffs and Thinifers* and Antoine de Saint-Exupéry (my mother loved *The Little Prince* but I, to my father's pleasure, liked it a little less), and where people drink champagne and cognac and eat frogs and snails. And here, in Paris, is where Nahum Gutman, who wrote *Lubengulu King of Zulu* for us, studied art and where the sweeper switched trains like we do in Lydda, and it continued to Marseille, on the shores of the Mediterranean, right here.

"The Mediterranean, that's already our own sea," my mother said proudly. She said that in Marseille the sweeper, by now an old seafarer, boarded a smaller ship with a captain as tall as a mast and a cook as round as a barrel and sailed straight across the Mediterranean to Haifa, the very same Haifa we arrive at on our way from Jerusalem to Nahalal.

Thus, without knowing it, the sweeper did what Uncle Yeshayahu himself should have: it made aliyah to the Land of Israel. Even if it was sent there as the revenge of one brother against the other and not to clean the national homeland of the Jewish people, it had ascended to Israel. And although it neither felt nor understood this, this was an act of pioneerism: to be the first vacuum cleaner in the Jezreel Valley, perhaps the first among Jewish settlers in all of Palestine.

At the palace of the British high commissioner in Jerusalem there would certainly have been a vacuum cleaner, but—and this "but" was uttered with slight scorn and patronizing disregard for the high commissioner's highness, his commissionership and his palace—it would have been English, which is to say, smaller and weaker than the American sweeper belonging to Grandma Tonia, so how could they even be compared?

Since the sweeper had reached the Land of Israel, we said a pleasant good-bye to the globe, took our leave of it, and returned to Brawer's atlas. The yellow pencil, too, took its leave from the enormous oceans and giant distant continents and returned to the "Map of the Lower Galilee and the Valleys" with which both it and I were quite familiar, where it could pinpoint Haifa Bay.

At the Haifa port the sweeper was off-loaded to the pier and at once understood that it was no longer at the port in New York or Rotterdam, and not even Marseille. It felt a sharp heat and smelled piquant scents, heard strange sounds and words and, of course, there was the dust, the enemy it was designed and produced to fight, which had attacked its crate and managed to invade between the slats. It sensed the sly onslaught, the touch of a thousand flutters, but it was not at all taken aback. Dust, it thought; dust, of all things. I'll show you, it said in its heart of hearts. I'll suck you in and destroy you. And the dust continued to swirl in, then fall and settle, and deep down inside, in its myriad of tiny deep-down insides, it was terribly frightened.

Here, at Haifa port, the sweeper was awaited by yet another Makarovite whose name my mother did not know. He did what Makarovites do for one another all across the world: he helped. It was he who arranged for the sweeper to be off-loaded from the ship and taken through customs, as must be done for electrical appliances that move from one country to another, and it was he who then had it loaded onto a wretched cart hitched to a wretched horse and transported to the train station, and the sweeper once again offered silent thanks to Uncle Yeshayahu for padding and wrapping it so carefully and meticulously, for the ruts in the road were worse than anything it had encountered to date.

This is the place to note that unlike many other travelers in those days on their first trip to the east, Grandma Tonia's vacuum cleaner was not fearful or enchanted or repulsed and, in the way of large, strong creatures, was full of contented awareness of its own power and quiet self-confidence. What are heat and being knocked around and dirt and dust to me? it hummed to itself. Just give me some electricity and I'll show you what I know how to do.

The sweeper was removed from the cart at the station now known as Haifa East and loaded onto one of the carriages of a train that no longer runs, except in the memories of those who tell stories about it—the Valley Train. The train whistled weakly, moved ridiculously, and "called itself a train" in the words of my mother, "even though turtles passed it with no problem and on the inclines, even the snails, too."

The railway ran along the bed of the Kishon River, the very same river that carried off the chariots of Sisera and flooded the Jezreel Valley with swamps that Grandpa Aharon and his comrades drained. And so it was that for the first time in its history—the Kishon could not believe what was transpiring—after so many soldiers and pioneers and peddlers and kings, there was a vacuum cleaner traveling its length.

The yellow pencil moved between the river and the Carmel mountains, squeezed into a space at the foot of the Mukhraka peak until it opened up into the wide expanses of the Jezreel Valley. The engine was so happy that it let out a whistle and steam, and right away the tip of the pencil stopped on the Tel El Shamam station at Kfar Yehoshua, its point so sharp that it left a tiny hole in the middle of the letter kaf in "Kfar."

"And here," my mother said, "in Tel El Shamam, Grandma Tonia's sweeper was met by family representatives: our horse Whitey and our uncle Yitzhak."

16

I have already mentioned Uncle Yitzhak in these pages, along with his brother, Uncle Moshe, and perhaps their wives, Yitzhak's Haya and Moshe's Haya. They lived in Kfar Yehoshua, the nearby moshav, with their sons and daughters, two of whom were, like my mother, named Batya after the same

Tonia's parents

grandmother from Rokitno in Ukraine whom I never met but who I know to have been a woman of valor, tall and beautiful, and who died several years after her arrival in Palestine and was buried in Nahalal.

My mother loved her uncles Moshe and Yitzhak and their children very much, but nevertheless called them Kishuim, or "Zucchinis." This surprised me greatly. I knew she hated zucchini, and this nickname sounded pejorative to me. When I asked her why she used this nickname, she said it did not apply only to her family but to everyone from Kfar Yehoshua. I asked if this meant they were bad people, at which she laughed and explained that it was all due to the sharpened point of a pencil.

And so I will explain it to you, too: on the map I have already mentioned, the "Map of the Lower Galilee and the Valleys" in Brawer's atlas, there was not enough room to write "Kfar Yehoshua" and so it was abbreviated to "K. Yehoshua." In the mouths of the people of Nahalal, who were always on the alert for just such an opportunity, this became "Ki-shua" and its plural form, "Kishuim," a name that contained scorn, mockery, and superiority.

Many Nahalal farm families had friends and relatives in Kfar Yehoshua, and on the Sabbath these families visited one another. Sometimes the Zucchinis came to Nahalal and sometimes the people of Nahalal traveled to Zucchiniland. Where our family was concerned, everyone preferred the latter option. First of all, because in the homes of her brothers, Grandma Tonia was not anxious about filth that might infiltrate, so she was relaxed and pleasant and behaved differently than she did in her own home. And second, because of the trip itself through the fields with a horse and cart. Years later, when I myself had come into the world and into the family, I took part in these visits a number of times and now, after having traveled to places far and remote, some of them under very rugged conditions, I can state unequivocally that as far as I am concerned, no journey has been as exciting and adventurous as those Sabbath visits to Uncle Yitzhak and Uncle Moshe. Immediately after the morning milking the family would dress in their Sabbath clothes, harness Whitey, place several sacks for people to sit on in the wagon, and set out for Kfar Yehoshua. The start of the trip is a long and gradual descent to the fields past the two palms of Ein Sheikha, the tall, straight one that is still there and the crooked one that buckled and fell. It was here that we heard once again the stories told by Grandpa Aharon of the draining of the swamps, and we all sang his song from those long-ago days when my uncles and aunt were small children like myself and set out on this very same journey. Menahem would brandish his whip at Whitey's backside and Grandpa Aharon would sing:

Oy, Menahem, spur the horse to hasten up the trip,
And if he does not wish to hurry, crack him with the whip!

Along the way my eyes followed wild animals, my true passion. I could always catch sight of Egyptian mongooses slinking across our path in their fiendish way and disappearing into the sheltering brush. During nesting season, spur-winged lapwings soared and dived above us, shrieking their piercing threats, while larks flew low in front of the cart, feigning injury so that we would be tempted to chase after them, leaving their silent chicks alone in their ground-level, camouflaged nests. Black snakes passed in front of us in the summer, fast and flickering like lightning, and if we were lucky, we saw that elegant bird, the northern lapwing, which is sometimes known by a funnier name, the peewit.

The climax of the trip was crossing the wadi, the ravine that in those days still had a little water flowing through it, where frogs and river crabs lived and wildcats caught tiny fish. Today, too, one can travel from Nahalal to Kfar Yehoshua through the fields, but on a tamed and proper gravel road leading to a low-water crossing built from cement in the wadi. Back then there was only a dirt path, and more than once the cart sank into the muddy riverbed. There was always a sense of concern before making the crossing, because if the cart sank then everyone would have to descend into the mud in their Sabbath clothes and push, and even then success was not guaranteed, so someone might have to run ahead and call for help.

Whitey himself did not love this wadi and was always hesitant before crossing it. It was as if he were pleading, "Maybe we can just forget this and go on back home?" or arguing, "Listen, people, we haven't exactly addressed the issue at hand, namely why it is that I am the only one who has to work on the Sabbath." However, despite all the affection and esteem the family had for Whitey, and their respect for his participation in the general effort at settling the Land of Israel, a horse must know his place. Grandpa Aharon chided him. Uncle Yair goaded him along with sounds made by clicking his tongue in his barely open mouth, sounds indescribable by consonants and vowels. I made clicking sounds, too, and it seemed that Whitey suddenly recalled the possibilities hidden between the lines of Grandpa Aharon's old song about Uncle Menahem and the whip, and he stepped forward against his will. His front legs muddied the water in the riverbed, then his back legs joined in. His large buttock muscles tensed. On the opposite bank, his horseshoes clung to the slippery incline and everyone shouted, *"Dee-yo!"* and, *"Udrub!"* in Hebrew and Arabic. Then we either succeeded or had to climb down from the cart to push.

After passing through the wadi we came to a long and gradual incline that led presently to Kfar Yehoshua, where we turned left. Whitey raised his head in joy and hastened his pace. He knew the trip was nearly over, while my own heart filled with worry due to the impending encounter with Uncle Moshe, who loved to kiss his guests and whom we called "the Kissing Uncle."

In Uncle Moshe's favor let it be said that he left no one out, swooping down on every family member he met. Men and women, adults and children—all were slathered with his kisses, which were big and strong and unavoidable. I recalled what my mother had told me on previous visits to Kfar Yehoshua and what she would no doubt repeat at any moment: "He is a very good uncle. Let him give you a kiss or two, then it's over—for you and for him."

Uncle Moshe and Uncle Yitzhak lived in two houses adjacent to each other and shared a common driveway—as did every two houses on the moshav—which split at the top when it entered the yards. Whitey, who already knew the way, turned from the road and then to the driveway, where a fascinating struggle ensued—a struggle that quite naturally can be told according to two versions. One has it that Uncle Yitzhak, who was better off than his brother, would offer a very nice meal of barley to Whitey while Uncle Moshe produced something a bit humbler, in keeping with his means. The other has it that Uncle Moshe was more compassionate and provided a generous meal to Whitey while Uncle Yitzhak was more strict and exacting than his brother. Whitey is the only one who knows which version is true, but he cannot determine the winner of this argument because he is dead. Still, back then he certainly remembered where the preferred meal could be had and always pulled to that side once he reached the split in the driveway.

Grandma Tonia, on the other hand, was always in the throes of a conflict with one of her brothers, each time a different one, the one she would call "my brother no longer." Whitey's meals held no interest for her, only her own matters. Which is why, on every such visit, she would press Whitey toward the yard of the one who happened to be serving as her brother that weekend. But Grandpa Aharon, who counted every penny and preferred that his horse eat the best free meal available, felt otherwise, and pulled the reins in the other direction.

Once, something terrible happened: Grandma Tonia pulled in Yitzhak's direction and Grandpa Aharon and Whitey pulled in Moshe's direction—or vice versa, depending on who is telling the story—and since Grandma Tonia was a strong woman, and her determination equal to that of two men (Grandpa and the horse), the plough shaft slammed into the concrete pillar where the driveway split and my uncle Yair, who was then a small child, flew from the cart into the space between the horse's back legs and the cart's front wheels and only miraculously was not trampled or run over.

The trip ended safely and we entered the yard. The uncles and their families came out to greet us, Moshe pressing ahead with lips puckered, Yitzhak hanging back, guarded and smiling pleasantly. The two were very different in appearance and demeanor. Moshe had thick hair and a sentimental, tempestuous heart. Yitzhak was quieter and more deliberate and his hair had already thinned. Moshe was a man of vision, aflame with ideologies, who wrote to David Ben-Gurion and Levi Shkolnik (later Levi Eshkol, Israel's third prime minister). Yitzhak was a practical man who invested wisely and with care. Often disputes would break out between them. But while they argued over family matters with Grandma Tonia, between themselves they fought "mostly over principles," not only their quality but their quantity, since, as my mother said, "Moshe had far more principles than Yitzhak, just like he had more hair on his head."

My mother told me that they had a special way of making up. They would run—literally—from Kfar Yehoshua to Nahalal because there was no time and lots of work to do, running the whole time next to each other but, in their anger, not sharing a word. They would stop running once they reached Nahalal because there they were joined by their sister, so rapid walking had to suffice. The three would go up to the cemetery where, on the grave of tall and beautiful Grandma Batya, they would hurl whatever they had at each other: claims and accusations and shouts and tears, and then they would hug and kiss and make up and cry some more, returning to the village at a clip. The brothers would then run back to Kfar Yehoshua, because there was no time and they had to get back to work.

"They didn't speak to each other on the way back, either," my mother said, ending the story.

"But they'd already made up," I said, perplexed.

"That's true," she said. "They'd made up and they were friends again, but they were tired and didn't have enough breath for both running and talking."

At Kfar Yehoshua we would eat a Sabbath breakfast, a large, late meal of fresh bread, salad, cheese, olives, and eggs and, occasionally, quivering squares of *kholodich*—calf's foot jelly teeming with lemon and garlic, a delicacy I love to this very day. These Sabbath breakfasts were similar to those of Nahalal, but quite different as well, if only in the way the vegetables were cut for the salad, or the size of the frying pan, or the type of bread, or the way the cheese was prepared.

Moshe's Haya and Yitzhak's Haya sliced bread just as Grandma Tonia did, clutched to the breast. Their movements, like hers, were strong and sure, but I feared the knife would wound them and once even said, aloud, "Be careful, Grandma, watch out for the knife," which made everyone laugh. Uncle Yair reassured me that I was wrong: "The knife has to watch out for Grandma, not the other way around," he said.

The Sabbath breakfast was a flow of stories, political arguments, conversations, and reminiscences—about movements like Hapo'el Hatza'ir and Poalei Zion; about muzhiks and kulaks, Ukrainian peasants and the "landed gentry" of the colonies; about the various Labor parties, Mapai and Mapam and Achdut Haavoda; about hired workers and mutual aid; and about less explosive topics as well, like orchards: prune at two knots or three. Or cowsheds: two daily milkings or three. But more than anything my older relations enjoyed arguing about who said what to whom and who did what to whom in family lore.

The laughter and shouting and tales were washed down with scalding tea poured from two kettles, a large one filled with boiling water and a second, sitting atop the first, filled with concentrated tea. "The jar of tea shall not be spent," my grandfather would say, paraphrasing a verse from the book of Kings that Moshe would complete: "Neither shall the cruse of concentrate fail." The two kettles provided many steaming liters of tea that doused our throats and ignited argument after argument.

Two types of sweets were served with the tea: one was *varenya,* a chunky jam chock-full of whole pieces of fruit, usually grapes. (Who had money for strawberries? my aunt Batsheva pointed out when she read a draft of this book.) The other was "herring tails," as my grandfather called herring, which was to him—and now to me—better than any sweet the world over.

Grandpa Aharon called it *selyodka* and told the following story about it: In the shop that his family had "back there" in Makarov, in Ukraine, "we sold products for the body, products for the soul, and products for between the two." When I asked him what he meant by that, he explained. "Products for the body were axes and hoes and boots for the Ukrainian farmers. Products for the soul were tallises, tefillin, and prayer books for the Jews."

Then he fell silent and stared at me in order to get me to ask what the products in between the two were.

"Grandpa," I said, "and what were the products in between the two?"

"In between the two," he chuckled, "is *selyodka,* herring. It's for both the body and the soul."

That is how everyone ate and drank and told stories and laughed and got angry and argued—everyone, that is, except Grandma Tonia, who had no time to waste, often taking Moshe or Yitzhak off to the side for a secret conversation in order to complain to them about what had been done to her or what had been said to her. She did the same with Moshe's Haya and Yitzhak's Haya.

In spite of the barrage of kisses from Uncle Moshe, I preferred meals there to those at Uncle Yitzhak's because at Moshe's the conversations were more interesting, more animated, and the stories more passionate, and also because Moshe accepted me as I was, which is to say he did not criticize me for being afraid to ride horses or grapple with calves. He did not slight me for failing to possess the technical skills of a typical son of farmers from Nahalal and even appreciated the interest I had already then in stories and books and the Bible.

Despite his devotion to Socialism, he also did not make comments on my father's citified manners or his past in the Etzel, the right-wing National Military Organization, because he admired my father's poems—unlike Uncle Yitzhak, who once made it clear to me that with a Revisionist father with two left hands I would never be a true moshav man. I was insulted, since as a child I thought being a moshavnik was a great achievement, a worthy aspiration for any man. But years later, when I was an adult and Uncle Moshe was dead, I went to visit Yitzhak at his home. He no longer worked his farm or apiary; instead, he spent long hours building astonishingly precise models of the wagons and plows and farm buildings that he remembered from his childhood in Rokitno.

He showed them to me one after the other, referring to them by the old Russian names that even today's Russian speakers probably are not familiar with, and told stories and reminisced. Over the years he had grown slightly gentler and more pleasant in his behavior and appearance. Time had removed the color from his face, but his gleaming eyes were even bluer, and they lit up the pallor of his years. For better or worse, old age works wonders on those who reach it.

17

When my sister was two or three years old our mother began to travel with us from Jerusalem to Nahalal by train: Jerusalem to Lydda, Lydda to Haifa, from Haifa a bus to the Nahalal junction, and then by foot or by catching a ride on a horse-drawn wagon.

Those journeys were less exciting than traveling with Motke Habinsky in the village tanker, and far shorter than the trip made by the vacuum cleaner, but they still had their own thrills. My father, who was more of a worrier than my mother, insisted on dispatching us to the train station in a taxi, and I recall words passing between them over the waste of money. He would come with us in order to help her board the train, and to bid us farewell as one did before a journey in those days.

The train station was on the other side of Jerusalem. We would leave the house at dawn, traversing unfamiliar neighborhoods, and board the train using a metal ladder consisting of three levels. My mother would board first with my sister in her arms, quick to find seats on the left side of the carriage. My father would then board with the suitcase and help me climb up. He placed the suitcase in the rack above the seats and scrutinized the faces of the other passengers to discern whether there were any "unpleasant people." Concerned but smiling, he whispered something to my mother, kissed her and us good-bye, and alighted, waving to us from the platform as we waved from the window.

The stationmaster's whistle sounded, the engine wheezed and sighed and began to move, and within minutes our window became the frame of an unfamiliar landscape, as if we had crossed an unseen border and traveled to a different land.

The first trains of my childhood were pulled by steam engines, and I can recall their pleasant, beautiful whistle and the loud, creaking protests made when the metal wheels met curves and bends. No one yet knew that in America someone had invented something called "air-conditioning." All windows were open and ash particles spewed by the engine borne by the wind blew straight into the carriage.

The trip started with a descent to the Refa'im stream, which we knew from stories our father told us about King David, then on to Soreq stream, familiar from stories about Samson. At that time, Refa'im served as the border between Israel and the Kingdom of Jordan. Our mother pointed out the Arab farmers on the other side as they worked small, neat plots of vegetables and watered them with the Jerusalem sewer water that ran in the ravine.

The train traveled slowly, and I was glad we were sitting on the left side of the carriage, facing the farmers. We waved hello and several waved back. The tracks were right on the border; each morning they were traversed by a lone carriage carrying several sappers on the lookout for mines and bombs, and in the first and last carriages of our train sat several armed border patrolmen. Nonetheless, there is something about train travel that fosters friendliness. And anyway, our mother said, "They're farmers like we are, so wave hello."

A man with two large pails filled with snacks came through the carriage, announcing that he had *"sanvishes,* drinks, gum, and cakes" for sale. But she never consented to buy anything from him. "We don't have money for that," she stated simply. "And our sandwiches are far better than his *sanvishes."*

The sandwiches she prepared and brought with us were made of dark bread spread with margarine, fried egg, slices of tomato, and leaves of parsley, and sometimes bits of cucumbers she had pickled. She explained something very important to us, which I observe to this very day: "One does not salt a sandwich when it is made. Instead, you bring a little salt from home and sprinkle it just before eating. That way the salt doesn't have a chance to turn the tomato into mush." We brought salt wrapped in a piece of newspaper, used it to salt our sandwiches, then ate them. We drank juice concentrate from the bottles we took to kindergarten and school.

At Hartuv we emerged from the hills to the plains. All at once the view widened and the curves straightened. The train whistled and hastened its pace. There were no more screeching wheels and the juddering of the train attained a certain rhythm and flow. Although it was forbidden, my mother allowed me to stick my head and arms a little way out the window, and the wind drew smiles on my face. The speed—which could not have been more than seventy or eighty kilometers per hour—made my head spin.

In Lydda we alighted and waited to board a different train bound for Haifa. I felt anxious: Maybe we had missed it. Or maybe the train to Haifa passed along some different route. Or maybe it would come but would stop for only a moment and we would not have time to catch it now that Father was no longer with us to help with the bags and suitcases. Maybe only our mother would manage to get herself onto the train while my sister and I would be left behind in Lydda for the rest of our lives.

But the train came on time and stopped pleasantly and we boarded pleasantly and traveled pleasantly to Haifa. Everything was slower then, the trips longer, and our mother moved from storytelling to quizzes to songs. She made up odd games, too. For example, we had to guess the names of all the people in the carriage, tell why those were their names, guess where they were going and why, what their jobs were, and other things about them as well. And all this we performed quietly so that no one would overhear us or catch us staring or pointing at them. Do not point at people. Stop that at once!

The train passed through the Rosh Ha'ayin and Eyal stations and we glimpsed the Arab towns of Qalqilya and Tulkarm, also on the other side of the border. The train tracks then were east of where they are now; it was only after the Binyamina station that the train approached the coast, and I was glad my mother had taken pains to find seats for us on the left side as our window filled with sea and sky, a most special and sensational view for a Jerusalem boy. Soon the first houses of Haifa came between us and the sea, and I envied their occupants for having sea and waves in their windows every day of the year.

The buildings of Haifa grew closer and closer to one another and became so crowded together that they hid the sea. The train whistled again and again, then slowed down and stopped with a great sigh at the Plumer Square station, and once again I was jealous of the residents of Haifa since the platform of their British-built station was as tall as the train's threshold, so there was no need to climb and descend scary metal ladders as there was in Jerusalem's Turkish-built station. We walked to the small Haifa Central Bus Station and caught an Egged bus to Afula that let us off on the main road, at the Nahalal junction.

From there we proceeded on foot on a scorching dirt path that passed between dusty casuarina trees. I moaned and complained about being thirsty and tired, about the heat and the heavy bag I was carrying. When we walked from our Kiryat Moshe neighborhood in Jerusalem to Grandma Zippora's flat in the Number 2 Workers' Housing Units in Rehavia and I complained of being thirsty, my father taught me that sucking on a pebble would wet the mouth and the thirst would pass. My mother had her own solution, which amused her greatly—and me, less: she would bring her cupped but empty hand to my lips and say, "Drink!" And then, "Drink more, you haven't drunk enough."

Now she said, "Drink from your bottle. That's why we brought it."

"But the juice is as hot as tea."

"If it bothers you that much then you can't be all that thirsty."

Although she was carrying a bag and a suitcase as well as my sister, her step was energetic and her carriage as erect as ever. She was happy to be entering the village. I have already written here that she was short in stature like her mother but her gait was light, which is how she walked there in spite of the long journey and the fatigue and the silent, heavy afternoon heat of the Jezreel Valley.

"Stop whining," she said. "In a little while someone will come by with a wagon and give us a ride."

Sure enough, almost always some farmer would pass by in a cart and give us a ride to the village. And even though the farmers were different, the same things always happened: he would call out to my mother, "Shalom, Batyaleh," and slow his horse, while she, as she walked, would toss the suitcase onto the moving cart, place my sister on it, and say to her, "Sit there and don't move; I'll join you in a moment," and then she would put my bag and her own on either side of my sister before taking a running start and then leaping onto the wagon in a most practiced manner that I envied. Each time, this took me by surprise, even by the time I could understand that this was a movement that every village dweller in those days, who had grown up with horses and carts, performed daily.

I was always left for last on the road, the farmer already clucking his tongue to get the horse going while my mother called out to me to do the same. "Run! Run! Get your feet moving or you'll stay behind, alone." Then she leaned over and thrust in front of me a smiling face and two hands, and I girded my loins and ran like Elijah the prophet beside Ahab's chariot, barely able to reach the large back wheel—which was taller than I—as it spun and murmured so close by. I raised my hands to hers so that she would catch me and pull me to her. For a brief moment I soared through the air and then I was with her, breathing hard, not quite able to calm down from the fear and the effort but sitting like her, my legs dangling over the edge, the ground blurry from small clouds of dust flowing past like a rapid stream, the agreeable scent of straw and dust rising to my nose.

My sister cast a scornful gaze at me while the farmer, who remained unimpressed at the small family drama that had taken place behind his back, would ask, "So what's new with you in Jerusalem?" and he would recount that he had read a poem by my father in Friday's *Davar* newspaper, and add the latest news from the village: someone who had received a ticket from the traffic cop at the checkpoint in Haifa, and the dog that would need to be put down because it had been infected with rabies by a jackal, and the latest "runoff" by my grandfather. My mother did not respond but she reddened from her neck to her forehead.

We arrived at the center of the village, where we would alight from the cart, say good-bye to the farmer—"And say good-bye to the horse as well!"—and then walk to Grandma's house. Here was the row of cypress trees, here was Grandpa Aharon's special citrus tree, here was Grandma's sack of dripping cheese, and here was Grandma herself, embracing us and saying, "Oy, Batyaleh, how good that you're here, maybe you could just . . ." And as was her wont, she would append a demand and a request, and soon she was complaining about everything that had been done to her recently. "You have no idea what he's done now . . ."

She had great admiration for my mother. More than once she asked her to intervene on her behalf, and when family problems erupted she would always postpone dealing with them, as she put it, "until Batya comes." In other words, Batya will come, she will pass judgment, she will dispense advice. Today as well, long after my mother has passed away, we still say "until Batya comes" quite automatically, then smile abashedly.

"How about if we go inside?" my mother said to her mother while instructing me to see what was happening in the yard. She did not want this conversation to take place outside, or in my presence. But to Grandma, it did not matter. It would not hurt her grandson to know what was being done to his grandmother by her neighbors, her children, her husband, her brothers.

I made myself scarce but stayed around to listen to every word. My curiosity extended beyond the stories my grandmother told to the stories told about her, mainly the ones told by my mother and Aunt Batsheva. First of all because they were more familiar than anyone with their mother's cleaning madness, and secondly, because I was always closer to the female members of the family. I loved their stories, the give-and-take of their conversation, their physical closeness, the tasks they tackled, the way I resembled them and they me. Most of the men of the family are as tall as Grandpa Aharon or taller, while my uncle Yair and I are short like the women, my grandmother, my mother, her sister, my sister, and my daughter—only Grandma Batya, as I have mentioned, was "tall and beautiful"—and even the shape of my body is similar to theirs, so much so that until I entered adolescence and my body grew strong and I began to work the farm with Menahem and Yair I actually felt that I was one of them, and that was a strange feeling.

Apart from this sense of belonging, and the fact that to this very day I know how to wring a floor rag the way the women do, this special kinship granted me many very interesting moments. While the boys of the family and the village were off wrestling and driving and fixing tractors, while they were firing guns and setting dogs on cats and riding horses, I would sit on the stoop of Grandma Tonia's porch and listen to her stories, each one beginning with that "This is how it was":

"This is how it was: I was a young girl who did not know the ways of the world . . ."

"This is how it was: he threatened to throw himself in the Jordan River . . ."

"This is how it was: Your mother was sitting on the platform shining the shoes of all the members of the family when suddenly a big, huge snake came slithering up to her. And she—she didn't even budge. She waited until it passed, then brought that big shoe brush down on its head. Wham! And she killed it."

Grandma Tonia also had stories that began with the phrase "When I was a girl," which in turn became a family expression used by anyone about to bring up old memories. When she used those words I knew there would soon be snow and ice, wolves, sleighs, and berries. A forest. A river. She told about the red and white sands of Rokitno and about the ateliers where colored glass was made from it, and about her studies at the gymnasium, which made her very proud, and about train trips so long that they had no end, and about the tall and handsome Russian officers who "winked at me in the train," and about family gatherings around the samovar where they drank dozens of cups of scalding tea, and about how the family would make jams and preserve fruit and prepare barrels of cabbage and sacks of tubers and onions, without which it was impossible to survive the difficult winter. She also told of the exemplary cleaning that took place at the home in which she grew up—Grandma Batya's house—as if to say that her demands in the cleaning realm were not her own madness but rather a family tradition that she guarded zealously.

Many years later, when my books had been translated into Russian, I was invited to Moscow to talk about them before an audience of people who spoke the language of my grandmother and grandfather. It was there that I received a compliment unlike any I have received elsewhere: that although I do not write in Russian, I am a Russian writer. I told them this does not surprise me, since I was very much influenced by four great Russian storytellers: Nikolai Gogol, Vladimir Nabokov, Mikhail Bulgakov, and Grandma Tonia, whom you may not have heard of here in Moscow but who, like Gogol, told wonderful stories and was born and raised in Ukraine—he in a village called Sorochyntsi and she in a village called Rokitno, which sounded small and lovely in her accent.

18

The stories Grandma Tonia told about Uncle Yitzhak were the most interesting of all. He was one of the first beekeepers in the Jezreel Valley as well as an excellent builder and craftsman. Although he was an almost engineer, he planned and erected homes and buildings, and even built the water tower in Kfar Yehoshua with absolute professionalism. Furthermore, it is only fit and proper that Uncle Yitzhak and his talents should play an important role in the matter of the hero of this story, the vacuum cleaner in whose honor he had come, with Whitey, to the Tel El Shamam railway station near Kfar Yehoshua.

Grandma Tonia would recount that Yitzhak showed an aptitude for work and an understanding of tools from a very early age. When he was only two and a half years old he had begun to hammer nails into the wooden floor of their house. "They told him no, shouted at him, punished him—but nothing worked," she said in her thick accent. In the end, Grandma Batya allotted him one square meter of kitchen floor, which in the course of a week he turned into a sheet of metal from so many nail heads hammered so close together.

Their younger brother, Yaacov, had inherited their mother Batya's height and beauty but was dark like the other members of the family. Yitzhak was not as handsome as Yaacov but did inherit their mother's sea-colored eyes. Once, Uncle Yaacov was courting some "Haifa girl" whose parents feared he was not "our kind," and this is how it was: "We had to bring Uncle Yitzhak to meet them so they would see we have blue eyes in the family."

Uncle Yitzhak was the hero of other stories far more thrilling and frightening. She told how "Gypsies" kidnapped him when he was three years old. "Those Tziganes tied him up with ropes and put him in a sack and Czar Nikolai's police found him in the sack three days later, at the Fastov railway station."

Another time, in winter, when Grandma Tonia and her siblings were small children in faraway Rokitno, Yitzhak persuaded her to put her tongue on the faucet of the well in their yard, and this is how it was: her tongue stuck to the frozen metal and she could not remove it.

I felt a physical pain. My whole body shivered. I could not understand how she could sit here on her porch, under the hot sun of the Jezreel Valley, speaking to me, when she was back there in the snow and ice, her tongue glued to frozen metal.

117

"And then what happened?"

"They unstuck me."

"How?" I asked, apprehensive. I was imagining knives, tugging, shouting.

"Moshe saved me with a little warm water and a wooden spoon. But I still have a scar. Look." She stuck out her tongue and let me inspect it from up close.

In short, it was with good reason that Uncle Yeshayahu asked Uncle Yitzhak to greet the vacuum cleaner at the Tel El Shamam railway station, and not Uncle Moshe. He knew them both and understood that there are events requiring compassion and vision and there are events in which someone sturdy and reliable and clear-sighted and dexterous is preferable, someone to unload the crate from the train and place it on a wagon and bring it to Nahalal without incident and open it there in the proper fashion and without aid. And anyway, my mother said, Uncle Moshe was an even bigger idealist than Grandpa Aharon, and a sealed crate arriving from America would have aroused his suspicions.

Yitzhak had been in the know for several months. He had received a letter from Uncle Yeshayahu with all the details and his requests, had memorized the information and then hidden the letter in the cowshed without sharing it with a soul. When the time came, he told Grandpa Aharon that he needed Whitey for mating purposes, which is also what they told Whitey himself, "since Whitey was a smart and friendly horse, but when it came to keeping secrets, he was no good."

And so, "the train arrived and Uncle Yitzhak unloaded the crate with the sweeper onto the wagon and bound it with ropes tied in a 'trucker's hitch'—a special knot used by truck drivers for securing loads—then said, 'Dee-yo!' to Whitey and they set out over the fields toward Nahalal."

My mother described in detail the picture of how they looked—a picture neither of us had seen, but which I shall never forget: a wagon in the distance, a broad and level field, the white of a horse, the blue of eyes, the yellow of field stubble and pencils, and chaff, cornfield green. Not only the two of us, but no one else saw all this beauty, either. It was a hot midafternoon and the farmers had returned to their homes for a meal and a nap. Only years later, when the picture turned into words, did that field grow even greener and blue eyes sparkle like sapphires. The sun appeared, burnishing the horse until it shone.

Uncle Yitzhak gave no thought to all this. In the first place, he did not see the picture because he was inside it. And second of all, he was concentrating on other matters. His brain, beneath the bald head under the cap, was alert, practical, and inquisitive and was preoccupied with conjectures. He knew that inside the crate was hidden a large vacuum cleaner meant for his sister, but he felt bound to keep his promise to Uncle Yeshayahu, so although he had never seen a vacuum cleaner and his curiosity was piqued, he did not open the crate to have a look.

As for Whitey, he showed no interest in the contents of the crate, and in his heart he said he would have been happy if that pretext of mating had been more than just an ugly deceit—at his expense—between relatives toying with his emotions. That is what happens, he concluded, when you are the only member of the family who walks on all fours.

Before reaching the wadi, Yitzhak tested the ropes to make sure they were properly tightened and the crate was in place. The sweeper, which had already crossed wide rivers in the United States and Europe, found it hard to understand what there was to worry about here. This time, Whitey was able to pass through the muddy ravine with ease; he knew that when it was just he and Uncle Yitzhak, alone, there was no need for the usual drama.

The wagon passed by Ein Sheikha, the spring with the twin palms, made the long and gradual ascent to Nahalal, and arrived at the southwest entrance to the village, between the Rachlevsky and Yehudai farms. Yitzhak was just about to turn Whitey to the right, in order to reach our farm straightaway, the fifth on the right, but Whitey understood that the load he was carrying today on his cart was not just some bales of hay or bundles of feed. No such thing! This was something absolutely special, different from every other load carried by every other horse and mule in the valley before him. And since he had decided to glean a little enjoyment from the matter, to make up for the mating that had not taken place, and since he possessed the proper dramatic instincts, he decided to do something special in honor of the event, a kind of celebratory performance for the entire village. So instead of turning right, he turned left and pulled the wagon with the crate from America the entire way around Nahalal. And Uncle Yitzhak, who was usually practical and thrifty and did not make unnecessary journeys, understood his wish and let him do what he wanted.

It is important to remember that the time was two o'clock in the afternoon. As I have already mentioned, the folks of Nahalal had finished their noon meals and gone off to nap as was customary before returning to work. But the sound of the horse's hooves in the silent and empty street caused them to awaken, and people sensed that something special was afoot, something that pulled even the weary ones and the principled ones and the inflexible ones from their beds, even the ones who had no time or interest in anything that was not related to security or agriculture. They all came out and regarded the crate and exchanged glances and scratched their heads and made guesses and wound up leaving home and following the wagon in a procession of the curious that grew and grew and grew.

An observer of this scene might have thought he was looking at some strange funeral procession, the coffin replaced by a large wooden crate covered in captivating foreign stamps and stickers from faraway ports and railway stations. And above all these, that puzzling, surprising inscription:

ƎNITSƎ˥∀d

˥∀˥∀H∀N

∀NIOꞱ ∀Ʇ∀∀S

No, this was no mistake—there was another, even more puzzling, instruction:

dՈ ƎᗡIS SIHꞱ

Fortunately, a few of the founders of Nahalal had come to Palestine after several years of working in the United States. They understood at once what had happened and stopped the cart. They translated what was written for Uncle Yitzhak and helped to undo the ropes and carefully upend the crate, hoping that no disaster had befallen—or perhaps hoping that some disaster had indeed befallen—its contents. No one knew what was inside, but it was clear that whatever it was had traveled from the Kfar Yehoshua railway station to Nahalal with its head down and its legs in the air like a scallion!

The people who knew English translated for those who did not and explained that this is the way things were done in America, that in spite of their shortcomings, Americans had some good traits that included pragmatism and thoroughness. But what it was that was hidden in the crate—this they did not know how to explain, even the ones who had lived in the United States. It was clear to all that the crate contained something suspicious and special, since the dim and seductive radiance of luxury goods was already gleaming through the cracks between the boards. All those gathered secretly began to plan how they would react and what they would say when they saw its source. In the meantime they decided that first they would see and then they would decide what to do.

Whitey, who was enjoying every minute of this, wished to circle Nahalal a second time, but Uncle Yitzhak pulled his reins and said, *"Hoysa!"* which is "Whoa!" to Hebrew-speaking horses, and, "That's as far as we go, comrades!" to all those who had escorted him, and he stopped the cart in front of his sister's home.

Grandma Tonia and Grandpa Aharon came outside with their children—Micha, Batya, and the twins, Menahem and Batsheva. They were so completely taken by surprise that they left the house by way of the front door and not the "second door," as was proper. Incidentally, Uncle Yair was not yet born, but as is customary in our family, he too can describe the event down to the last detail.

Grandpa Aharon caught sight of the English writing on the crate and at once understood that this time his brother had come up with something truly villainous. He stood rooted to the spot, so it was left to Nahum Sneh, his friend from the glorious Makarovite Trio of the Second Aliyah, to offer assistance to Uncle Yitzhak.

The two grabbed hold of the wooden crate, took it down from the wagon, and carried it around the house to the platform, where they set it down. Uncle Yitzhak, who was never caught without his tools and had brought with him an entire tool kit, pulled out a screwdriver and a claw hammer while Nahum Sneh stood by in order to intercept any threat or calamity. Who knew what might pop out of such a crate, what terrifying, tempting ogre, sent as it was from America?

My mother had clear recall of that day and could list everything that happened from the moment the crate was opened:

The nails were removed with a screeching sound and were gathered and saved for future use.

The metal straps were placed to the side for future use.

The wooden slats were broken down and arranged one atop the other for future use.

The special American light that got trapped in the crate when it was sealed in the United States had grown slightly brighter and sent out scouting rays that mixed with the strong Land-of-Israel light outside the crate.

"And what was discovered inside the crate⸮" she asked.

"The sweeper, the vacuum cleaner!" I said joyfully.

"Not yet. First of all, they found a box."

Riveted into place and surrounded by padding in the form of crumpled American newspapers, rags, and sawdust was a large cardboard box bound with a thin, strong, white rope and printed—here my mother's voice filled with amusement—with a drawing of something unfamiliar but clearly upside down, its head pointed to the ground and its legs in the air, as we have said, like a scallion!

"*Nu, nu,*" said everyone who had not passed through the United States en route to the Land of Israel, and Uncle Yitzhak breathed a sigh of relief. Apparently those Americans were not as thorough as believed and were capable of making mistakes. The sweeper had traveled from America to Kfar Yehoshua upside down, and from Kfar Yehoshua to Nahalal right side up! Because that's the way Uncle Yitzhak was: he may not have known English but he was an almost engineer and he knew how to put everything in its proper place.

He took out the sharp jackknife given to him by Grandpa Aharon after Aharon taught him how to graft fruit trees. He cut through the straps that held the box in place and turned it over, causing everyone gathered to gasp with fear, for now it was possible to identify the picture on the box. It seemed to be that of an American housewife—one, in fact, of many like her—the devil in the image of a woman, her lips bright with red lipstick, a red polka-dot dress snug on her hips, an ample bosom, meaty buttocks. Her nails were painted with red nail polish. It was clear to one and all: she has her hands manicured!

The box was so large that the woman in the picture was nearly life-size, which is to say, Grandma Tonia's height. And most important of all, she was not alone. In her hands she held a long, thick tube that extended from some sort of large appliance on wheels, which was pictured crouching obediently at her feet. Not everyone understood what the nature of this appliance was, but they did understand that it was residing inside the box. Most especially they understood that everything they had ever thought about America up to that very moment did not even reach the shapely ankles of this woman, every detail of whose image attested to pampering and coquetry and frivolity and hedonism and the sanctity of individualism. Regard and ponder this: What luxury good was this appliance that could bring such a shameful smile to the red, red lips of this woman?

The women and men of the village, the beasts and the fowl, the fruitless shade trees and the fruit-bearing trees alike—all were scandalized. Cries of derision could be heard—"Coquette!"—as well as cries of wrath and shock: "For shame! Shame and disgrace!" But today I understand what my mother did not recount—that these pioneering men were still men, and in the way of men they had already thought several thoughts in their heart of hearts about those hips and what they would mean to a pair of hands accustomed only to work. And the women regarded this woman on the box with scorn, but at the same time wondered what it would be like to be such a woman. Some of them were jealous. Why her? And others licked their lips and pressed them shut without realizing it. Most notably, not a soul left the scene. No one averted his eyes, or hers. They were scandalized as was only proper and fitting, but they stood waiting for more.

Only Grandma Tonia was not scandalized. First, because the village constitution and the principles of the movement had never interested her. And second, the box had been sent to her and its contents were intended for her and the woman on the box seemed at once like a cohort, an ally, a woman wholly absorbed with cleaning, albeit one with appliances and tools that enabled a kind of cleaning that could not yet even be imagined here in Palestine.

And there was something else she felt, a magical, secret sensation that fluttered about the edges like an embroidered hem that borders an expensive tablecloth: that she could have been a woman much like this one, happy and joyous, even made up and colorful in a polka-dot dress, if she had married a double traitor like Uncle Yeshayahu or maybe even Uncle Yeshayahu himself and not his brother Aharon, and she had traveled with him to America instead of this dirty and demanding Palestine.

Uncle Yitzhak was also imagining and wondering and wished finally to open the box and have a look inside. But Grandma Tonia shook off her dreams and returned to her senses and instructed him first and foremost to remove from the crate all the rags that had padded the box and bring them to her. Even if a state-of-the-art appliance had come from America she would always find use for these American rags, which she had noted at once were of a far higher quality than the ragged rags used in the Land of Israel.

Yitzhak collected the rags and handed them to her, and she felt a great sense of satisfaction. She did not yet know what was inside the box, but at least she had already received one gift from America.

19

Most of this story I heard in Jerusalem, along with the other stories my mother told about her family. But some of the details were added and became clearer to me when we moved to the place where it all happened, Nahalal.

This chapter of my life—highly significant, though short—began when I was nine years old. My mother had had it with being a housewife, and the mortgage on our modest apartment was too burdensome for the salary of one teacher with a family to support. At the time, there was a teacher's seminary in Nahalal that offered an intense and accelerated study program, so we went to live there. My mother studied at the seminary and my father taught at the agricultural high school in the village.

The chance to live near Grandma Tonia, Grandpa Aharon, and my uncles Menahem and Yair excited me and filled me with joy. I loved them, and the yard, and the cows and calves, and Whitey, and the fields and the birds, especially the chicks in the chick run. I even liked the geese, which would attack and peck at me. All of these had a double presence in my consciousness: a strong literary presence that my mother had implanted in me while we still lived in the city, and a real-life presence nurtured by our many journeys to the village and now strengthened by our going to live there.

My parents rented the second floor of the Karasik family home, not far from Grandpa Aharon and Grandma Tonia's house. The apartment consisted of only two rooms and a small hallway, but they were more spacious than those of our tenement building in Jerusalem. The room I shared with my sister had a panoramic view of the fields to the southeast and an out-size, sun-drenched porch that could be accessed by climbing out the window over my bed.

We moved there at the beginning of the summer holidays, and to everyone's surprise and pleasure the relations between my father and my grandmother improved—which is to say, they became tolerable. She even came to visit us often. My father would hear her on the stairs and say, "*Hamati olah,*" a play on words that could mean "my mother-in-law is coming up the stairs" or "my fury is rising." But he said this with a smile, not in anger.

And something else good happened. In Nahalal my sister and I had our first dog, a mixed terrier we got from friends whom we gave the very original name of Lucky. He was a smart and happy puppy who grew to become a real member of the family. One winter day our mother played a trick on him, dressing him in a blue wool pullover she was knitting for my sister. We all laughed and Lucky was completely humiliated. He ran outside with the blue pullover on him and my mother dashed out after him. She chased him for an hour in the mud and rain, escorted by a pack of excited and gloating village dogs, until at last she returned, waving the wet and filthy pullover, a victorious expression on her face. "That was all we needed," she said, breathing heavily. "Now they'll say about us in the village that we knit sweaters for dogs." My mother was laughing, but when she said "they'll say about us in the village" she was dead serious.

She tried to get me interested in farmwork but without much success. Uncle Menahem had given her a small plot of land behind the chicken coop and she planted cucumbers, peppers, eggplant, garlic, onions, and tomatoes for family consumption. Every day after her studies she would go out there to work and it was not long before she asked me to help her.

I went willingly. We weeded and cultivated and hoed, but after half an hour I straightened up, leaned on my hoe, and told her, "Now you work and I'll tell you stories."

She burst out laughing, but others ostracized me, recalling my father's cucumber fiasco. Several years later I began working with Menahem and Yair more seriously, and even enjoyed myself. But at the time, when I was nine, I showed none of the diligence expected from someone who wishes to be crowned "the son of farmers from Nahalal." I was quite content with morning visits to the cowshed, to which my sister and I were dispatched in order to bring milk home.

There was always loud music playing in the cowshed because Uncle Menahem had hooked up a loudspeaker that fed from the radio in the house. He said the music had a positive effect on the amount of milk that the cows gave, as well as on its quality. Whenever he wanted to switch from the Voice of Israel to Army Radio or vice versa, he would stick his fingers in his mouth and whistle loudly; his wife, Penina, could hear his whistle in the house and would move the dial to the appropriate station. While milking, Menahem and Yair would argue between themselves, mimic people, and tell tales about their parents or the neighbors or themselves and everyone else in the village.

To my mother's great pleasure, from the uncles I learned more and more family expressions, most of which were Grandma Tonia's inventions, and I began to use them. In particular I liked "I am shaking all over" (when she wished to express great anger), and "When I was a girl," which I have already mentioned, and "I am *broked* in body and spirit."

And most especially I liked what she would utter whenever someone died (and always in the feminine, even if it was a man who had died): "She is no longer," to which she would add, "and it was a terrible death." These were not exactly mistakes of grammar or medicine; they were her linguistic inventions, which the family adopted with glee. Still today we say, "She is no longer" for men and women alike, and for cars wrecked in accidents, to which the pedants add, "and it was a terrible death," even when the person's passing was a gentle kiss of death at a ripe old age.

Some of my grandmother's expressions spread among family friends as well, and one of her sayings even became a global classic. This was the expression *"At ponit elai?"* Imagine our excitement when, many years later, we watched the film *Taxi Driver,* and there was Robert De Niro looking at himself in the mirror as he practiced gun-slinging and used an exact translation of that expression: "You talkin' to me?"

Personally, I was not surprised, because I knew how that line had made its way from Nahalal to faraway Hollywood, but the rest of the family was astonished. Everyone phoned everyone else just to ask, imitating Grandma Tonia's particular way of speaking, whether they had seen *Taxi Driver,* because she had begun saying "You talkin' to me?" long before Robert De Niro, even if it was in Hebrew and with a Russian accent. And unlike the taxi driver, who practiced saying it in the secrecy of his room, with a drawn gun in front of a mirror, Grandma Tonia said it in the center of Nahalal to her enemies' faces, empty-handed. "You talkin' to me?" she would mutter with contempt before turning around and walking away with all the pride she could muster with her short body and legs.

After school and lunch I would go to Yair, who was and still is my closest uncle. Yair is older than I by only eight years, so we were more like brothers than uncle and nephew. He was the old-age child of his parents and grew up at a time when relations between them were worse than ever. His older brothers and sisters were already grown-up and married and out of the house and he was lacking the support they gave one another as children. However, he had—and still has—a life preserver in the form of a great sense of humor, and we enjoyed ourselves

Tonia, Yair, and Aharon

together, and spoke to each other like an older brother and younger brother.

Once, a mysterious predator was stalking the chicks in our run, killing dozens; well beyond satiety, it seemed to be killing simply out of bloodlust. Yair had a .22-caliber rifle, known as a "tutu," and was an outstanding marksman. He decided to stage an ambush to catch the culprit—assumed to be either a weasel or a wildcat—and invited me to join him.

When night fell we took our places facing the chick run. We lay waiting in utter silence. Yair forbade me from talking or moving so as not to make the predator suspicious. After a while I fell asleep and was jolted awake an hour later by the single shot he fired. He hit that predator, in complete darkness, right between the eyes! We felt our way to the culprit, a big yellow house cat that had gone feral, or perhaps a crossbreed between a wildcat and a house cat that had gone out for a stroll in the fields.

The next morning Yair displayed his catch in a box in the yard "so that all the cats and weasels and jackals know not to mess with us," he explained to me. The cat remained there for a day or two and was then dumped at the edge of a field to become prey for birds of the sky and beasts of the earth, and the chicks in our run were no longer attacked.

Yair took his afternoon nap outside in a hammock strung between two citrus trees, a habit that made his mother very happy. This hammock was a faded mattress atop an old iron cot to whose corners Yair had welded chains. We would swing on that hammock and doze off in the afternoons when our bellies were full and our bodies tired and the earth gave off heat and the round-shaped Nahalal was like a giant frying pan.

At those hours of the day the village could be compared to a graveyard. Dogs panted in the shade. Chickens fainted in the coops. The young, inexperienced birds that mistakenly chose to fly just then tumbled from the sky and crumbled into dust on the ground. The humans slept deeply, resting up for late-afternoon work: moving irrigation lines, bringing hay from the fields, the night milking. Even Grandma Tonia stopped cleaning for two whole hours.

We hunkered down there, in my eyes like Huckleberry Finn and Tom Sawyer, and when Grandma Tonia's light, spiraling snores began, Yair would get up and steal into the kitchen to sneak out a large mug filled with cream and cocoa and sugar before his mother could notice, wake up, and take chunks out of him. Back in the hammock he would whisk it all up with a fork until it became like smooth whipping cream and we would eat it spoonful by spoonful.

I have been young and now am old but I have never tasted anything like that sweet treat again. In addition to the texture—the smoothness of the cream, the sensuality of the cocoa, the sweetness of the sin and the sugar—it also contained a proclamation of rebellion and independence. Just as the priests had controlled the meat market of the faithful who came to the Temple in Jerusalem during the days of the Bible, so too did the generation of founding fathers and mothers of Nahalal assume control over all things sweet, locking them away in drawers and hiding them on the highest shelves. They even forbade anything sweet from being distributed at the village store—not only due to shortage or savings but for moral reasons as well, so as not to corrupt the souls of the young, turning them into addicts. Once, an ice-cream vendor was chased from the village, but not before kerosene was poured into his box of ice creams so that he would never dare return with his trashy merchandise.

Grandma Tonia did not have such morals. As far as ideology was concerned she was more like her brother Yitzhak than her brother Moshe. Her considerations were always practical, not ideological, having to do with the family and not the movement. Grandpa Aharon, on the other hand, was in the habit of moralizing to his grandchildren every chance he had, though luckily he often did this by way of a story. When we asked for a candy he would tell a story from his childhood in Makarov, when they did not even have sugar, not to mention actual candies. He probably wished to implant feelings of guilt and regret for our unforgivable hedonism. But to his credit he did this by putting himself down and, unlike all sorts of professional complainers, who tell of the wealth and status they and their families enjoyed overseas and gave up to come to Israel, he actually told of poverty and paucity.

"We were so poor," he would announce, "that we all had to sweeten our tea with a single cube of sugar."

"Did you break it into pieces and divide it up?" I asked.

"No," he replied. "We tied it to a piece of string hanging from the ceiling and looked at it while we drank our tea."

Our most debauched and desired form of sweets was the

ice cream at Tel Hanan, near Nesher. By this time Uncle Micha was married to Aunt Tzafrira and they were living not far from Haifa, in Kiryat Haim. Each time we went to see them we stopped for Tel Hanan ice cream, as eager as a yeshiva boy on the prowl for a woman in a strange town. Uncle Menahem had a Triumph Standard at the time, a small and wretched junker that could seat four midgets. But he managed to cram himself, his wife, Penina, their oldest son, Zohar—who was my sister's age and who was later killed in the Yom Kippur War—their infant daughter Gila, Uncle Yair, my mother, my sister, and me inside the car, and sometimes even Grandma Tonia and Grandpa Aharon as well. The method was simple: first the adults climbed in and seated themselves, smashed together as best they could, then the children formed a second story on top of them.

We always encountered people hitching rides on our way out of the village. Menahem would stop the car next to them and shout, "Come on, jump in, there's lots more room in the car!" He held the steering wheel with his left hand and used his right hand for smoking and shifting gears. Even my mother, who did not yet have her driver's license, took an active role in the driving: She would stick her hand out the window to hold on to the small gas tank on the roof of the car, from which there was a tube leading straight to the carburetor. The Standard's fuel pump did not always work so we were at the mercy of gravity. And that is how we would drive, with no one complaining that it was crowded, because everyone wanted to visit Uncle Micha and Aunt Tzafrira and have a Tel Hanan ice cream on the way. Everyone, that is, but Grandpa Aharon, in whose eyes that ice cream was just another terrible luxury.

We lived in Nahalal for two years and two months, and the two grades I completed there—the fourth and the fifth—were the best of my childhood and youth. The Nahalal school was the finest school at which I studied; the teachers were excellent and open-minded and the lessons were often conducted outside, in the wadi, in the Shimron hills near the cemetery, in the woods and fields. But mostly I enjoyed the proximity to my mother's large and tempestuous family in all its colors and stories and memories and expressions and miseries and insults and joyful occasions and score-settling and emotions. When we returned to Jerusalem, to the gray cinder blocks of our tenement, to the city's mad and blind and orphaned, everything seemed gloomy and sick and depressed after the green-gold days in the village, days of sun and nature, of bodies exposed to fresh air, of bare feet on hot earth, of a boy and a dog and mysteries and stories behind locked doors.

20

Uncle Yitzhak opened the box and pulled something large and heavy from inside it wrapped in a thick, soft sack. The gleam grew stronger, very nearly bursting through the weave of the cloth. The gathered crowd murmured and moved closer, preparing itself for the light that would shine any moment, as soon as Yitzhak pulled away the sack and exposed it.

Uncle Yitzhak did not tarry. He pulled away the sack and exposed Grandma Tonia's sweeper to the eyes of the village. Jaws dropped. Eyes popped. Not everyone understood what they were seeing; there were those who thought this was some new kind of pesticide sprayer or a particularly elaborate milking machine of uniquely American invention, some automatic American milking machine that would follow cows through meadows. However, most of those present understood at once that this was yet another of those capitalist luxuries of the very worst kind, whose sole purpose is idleness and pampering. The bright glare from the chrome, the curvaceous body, the large wheels that attested to a fear of hard work—all these could not possibly coexist with the moshav constitution and its values, and the village comrades gritted their teeth, returned to their senses, and suppressed with iron fists whatever desire the object aroused.

Still, beneath it all, hearts pounded. Even in a society that is all values, those present could not deny what their hearts felt: that the truth could not be hidden. That with all that earth and labor and milk and vision, the shine and pleasantness and pleasure itself had vanished from their lives. That these hands that plow and harvest and build and milk wish to be idle on occasion, enjoy themselves, touch smooth hips. Fingernails ached and longed to be painted and cared for. Eyes that scanned for enemies and vermin all day long, that searched for proof of having chosen the right way, that scoured the heavens for even a single rain cloud, burned with desire and wished to shut with longing and pleasure, like my mother's eyes would shut so many years later when at long last she allowed herself a single weekly corruption, a small glass of Drambuie each Friday late in the afternoon between the cooking and the meal, and sometimes even her favorite delicacy, on Sabbath morning: real anchovies.

How surprising that she, scion of a herring-eating family and someone quite talented at making such herring herself, loved the taste of anchovy. When we were children she never bought anchovies because they were more expensive than we could afford, so instead she would bring home from our local Jerusalem grocery an anchovy substitute sold in a metallic yellow tube with a red cap. She would spread a thin layer on a thin slice of bread and top it with nearly transparent slivers of tomato, and before she took a bite she would say with mock importance, in a nasally, amused voice, "*Anchois.*" Which is to say, Here we are—the muzhiks, the peasants, the *selyodka*-eaters, the sons and daughters of farmers from Nahalal—tasting real anchovies at the court of the king of France, so take care, children, not to dirty your silken raiment, your muslin ruffs.

Later, when she could finally afford the real thing, she would eat her anchovies with a piece of challah bread and a cup of black coffee and enjoy herself, as she said, "like thirty pigs." But real anchovies never pleased my palate like that substitute had, because my mother never said "*anchois*" when she ate them.

The village comrades regarded the vacuum cleaner, and the vacuum cleaner stared back at them. What it saw was hardworking people, work clothes, and strong hands. Their appearance attested to lives of moderation, simple food, a clear path. There were such farmers, it knew, in its homeland of America, but back there such a life came from lack of choice while here—it understood at once—this was a matter of choice, a goal. There they went to work with stooped backs and lifeless eyes, while here Jewish farmers stood proud in their convictions.

For an instant, the vacuum cleaner wished to withdraw, to return to its soft and pleasant cloth covering, to close itself into the cardboard box and seal itself beneath the beautiful American woman; it was meant for this woman, or someone like her, no matter if she was standing on her legs or upside down like a scallion. But then it caught sight of Grandma Tonia: no narrow hips, no painted lips, no manicured hands, no red and tempting smile. But she did not stand before it like some pillar of salt; instead, she uprooted herself from the members of her family and walked toward it. The vacuum cleaner had found its mistress and their covenant: together they would fight against dirt and dust.

She touched it, and in spite of the chill of the metal she felt a pleasant warmth. At once she wiped off the fingerprint she had left behind with the rag draped over her shoulder and smiled in satisfaction. Then she took hold of the thick, serpentine tube, flexible and firm at the same time and tipped in sparkling metal, and when she lifted it into the air the sweeper moved toward her on its large, silent wheels that know no effort.

The vacuum cleaner moved so quickly and obediently that the crowd murmured in fear and awe. Grandma Tonia herself was slightly alarmed and took a step back, but the tube was in her hand so it was pulled along with her. She smiled and turned to the right and the sweeper, like some professional dancer, followed close behind so that when she turned left it turned charmingly with her.

There was something pleasant and uplifting about this picture, and something off-putting and frightening as well. Once again the crowd murmured and Grandma Tonia cried, "The show's over, people. There's lots of work to be done!" and with that she turned around and entered the house, and the sweeper, like some enormous pet that has just sworn loyalty to its owner—actually, why deal in metaphors when the reality is so clear: like a vacuum cleaner that understands that this is its mistress and this is its house and here is the place in which it will toil and clean from now on—followed her inside.

Only then, in the house, did Grandma Tonia allow herself to sit on a chair and breathe deeply. Grandpa Aharon said nothing. His face was dark and his hands shook. He took a good look at the huge appliance and understood the depth of his older brother's revenge. I believe it is safe to assume that in spite of the ideological and emotional struggle taking place inside him, he was also busy calculating the sum that would appear on his next electricity bill.

Uncle Yitzhak, on the other hand, had begun preparing for the initial running of the vacuum cleaner. First he checked that Uncle Yeshayahu had made sure to purchase a model that would work according to the wattage used by the British Mandate. Then he searched the box and found a smaller box, with the same picture of the woman in her polka-dot dress and painted nails and lips, but much smaller than her twin, and inside there was another cloth bag containing all sorts of plugs and converters, general proof of American thoroughness and specific proof of Uncle Yeshayahu's thoroughness, since he worried that the outlets in Palestine might not suit American plugs and did not wish to see his scheme fail due to trivial matters.

Everything was in place: the home built in Nahalal in the Jezreel Valley, the electricity that arrived from Naharayim in the Jordan Valley, the housewife from Rokitno in Ukraine, the vacuum cleaner sent from Los Angeles in the United States, and the dust of the Jezreel Valley, which was there from time immemorial and, like the dust of Haifa, felt fear in its myriad of tiny floating hearts.

Yitzhak was eager to break down the vacuum cleaner, scrutinize it to understand how it worked, then put it back together and explain to his sister whatever needed to be explained before putting it to its first test. But Grandma Tonia denied his request. "The svieeperrr is mine. It is ready and I know how to work it," she said. "It's very simple. In America everything is simple. It's only with you people that things are difficult."

She inserted the plug into the outlet in her home, and as if practiced and accustomed she pressed her foot to the large starter on the back. The vacuum cleaner obeyed, responding to her with a soft and confident purr. Grandma Tonia held the tube and off went the two of them to work. When Grandpa Aharon caught sight of the sweeper sent by his brother and his wife as she waved her new magic and wrathful wand at her old enemies he announced that he had a headache and decided to "runoff" again, but this time he only got as far as the orchard.

"Did she chase after and catch him?" I asked, using Grandma Tonia's accent.

My mother gazed at me with satisfaction. The child was learning both family lore and its language. "What do you mean, chase after him? She aimed the tube at him and the sweeper sucked him right back to her."

"No way! That's not how it was."

"All right. She didn't really suck him in, but she stopped him and pulled him in, and that's how she got him back in the house and sat him at the kitchen table."

"Sit here, Aharon," my grandmother said, and Grandfather sat, knowing he had been beaten.

"And then what happened?"

"I have no idea. When I went to bed they were still sitting and not talking."

That night, neither of them slept. They lay next to each other, their eyes open, boring into the darkness—he, from frustration and fury, she, from joy. He: the double traitor has won. She: the house will be cleaner and shinier than ever before.

In the morning, Grandma Tonia used the sweeper once again and this time she went over the floor with the flat head. When she finished, she examined the results by washing the floor, sponging up the water with a rag, wringing it into a bucket, dipping her hands into the water, and raising them up to watch the drops drip in the light. And they were clear as springwater, absolutely clear. She was rapturous. But later, after she had wiped down and polished her new sweeper with a rag, she felt that something was bothering her. Something unclear, a small problem that she could not ignore. Something, if I may use an image from her own world, was dirtying the clarity of her joy.

Next to the joy, or, to be more precise, next to the joy and just below her ribs, warning signs were throbbing. This is a feeling sensed by many without understanding the exact meaning, when the body comprehends some event before the brain does. The sweeper's efficiency was too perfect; the way it cleaned, faultless and effortless, aroused her suspicions. Something about this new appliance filled her with worry.

21

Human memory awakens and extinguishes at will. It dulls and sharpens actions, enlarges and shrinks those who perform them. It humbles and exalts as it desires. When summoned, it slips away, and when it returns, it will do so at the time and place that suits it. It recognizes no chief, no overseer, no classifier, no ruler. Stories mix and mingle, facts sprout new shoots. The situations and words and scents—oh, the scents!—encrusted there are stored in the most disorganized and wonderful manner, not chronologically, not according to size or importance or even the alphabet.

When I began writing this book I burrowed into my own memory and that of other members of my family. I wanted to know exactly what Grandma Tonia's sweeper looked like and hoped to clarify a few technical, factual details concerning it, but I was not able. My mother is no longer alive, and even when she was, I was aware that there was no believing every detail of every story she told. She loved and knew how to make things up; facts, to her, were nothing more than a small and boring obstacle that could be skipped over or made use of like a springboard. As for me, I did actually see the sweeper with my own eyes, but only one time, and in very strange circumstances about which I shall say only this at the moment: these were circumstances likely to affect both perception and memory.

Other family members recounted, as we are wont to do, their own versions, which sometimes conceal a clear bias and sometimes merely the need to be different. Thus, I used objective sources in my search for Grandma Tonia's sweeper. I did not find one certain model that I can point to as definitive, but I did find several interesting facts.

The first vacuum cleaner came into the world in 1869, decades before one of its descendants reached my grandmother. That was a manual model, not particularly efficient, that failed to create a market. Later, at the turn of the century, a huge and noisy mechanical vacuum cleaner was invented in England and transported from house to house on a horse-drawn cart and operated by an internal combustion engine. The enormous cleaner would be parked in front of the customer's home, and long tubes were stretched from it into the rooms while a team of cleaners operated it.

Even the royal palace ordered several visits, though not merely for the cleaning—there were certainly more than enough servants and rags available at Buckingham Palace for that—but rather as a sort of show for guests. So while these guests were ambling about the salons and gardens sampling cucumber sandwiches and sipping champagne and Pimm's, this monstrous creature appeared in the palace courtyard, dispatched its tubes inside, and began vacuuming. I have no idea whether it did a good job cleaning, but it was no doubt a riveting conversation piece for bored aristocrats.

The first electric vacuum cleaner was invented in 1907 by an Ohio janitor by the name of James Spangler, whose chronic asthma was worsened by the dust he encountered. Spangler attached an old fan motor to a soap box stapled to a broom handle with a pillowcase, and together they managed to suck in some of the carpet dust flying about the room. One of the first customers for his new invention was a cousin married to

William Hoover, a saddlemaker and leather merchant who took a commercial interest in Spangler's appliance. Hoover bought the patent, made Spangler a partner, made improvements to the vacuum cleaner, and came up with a radical new marketing idea: ten-day free home trials. His success was so enormous that within several years the name Hoover became synonymous with every vacuum cleaner in the world. Everywhere, that is, except for our family. To this very day we call every vacuum cleaner a sweeper, and of course with a Russian accent.

Still, not only the vacuum cleaner is of interest but also the dust it fights, the dust that provides meaning for its very existence. I have discovered that most of the dust in our homes, some 75 percent, is the dead skin cells and hair of the occupants and their pets. Which is to say that Grandma Tonia was right: people are better off staying outside. Let them sit on porches and shed their skin out there, not inside her house on the freshly washed floor!

It should be noted that this finding is true for American dust, where windows are closed and air conditioners filter in clean air and housewives have their hands manicured. But into Grandma Tonia's house—a single-story home with wooden shutters and window screens facing a dirt yard and open fields in a village in the Middle East—a very different type of dust infiltrated, motes of actual earth, a matter that Mr. Hoover could never have been familiar with or even imagined.

Quite a lot has already been said and written about the complex relationship between the Jewish pioneers and their soil, but with Grandma Tonia matters were even more complex. She knew something that Zionism tended to ignore: that the land was not simply virgin soil, the land of our forefathers, a foothold for persecuted and wandering Jews. Under certain circumstances, not at all unusual, it was merely dirt.

Jezreel Valley earth is heavy and fertile and takes on two forms: in summer, it is dust and in winter, mud. Which is to say that one way or the other, it is always dirt. In the early days of Nahalal there were no paved roads, nor were the yards covered with ground basalt and certainly not with cement. The winter mud was deep and heavy, so heavy that legs sunk in up to the knees and wheels to their axles. Boots went missing in it and small children were pulled through it on "mud sleds" made from wooden boards and tin. The mud smeared and stuck to everything, which is how it moved from place to place and entered right into the house. Years later, during my childhood there, we carried pairs of slippers in our schoolbags, which we put on after shedding our boots when we reached school. Even today, in the era of asphalt and mortar, you can still find mud-fighting weapons next to every house in every village in the valley: welcome mats for wiping one's feet, boot removers, and sole scrapers.

In summer, the earth dried up, so when the roads were stomped by horses' hooves and work boots and wagon wheels, and the fields by plow blades and the iron teeth of harrows, dust was created, a commando unit of determined and cunning infiltrators composed of motes of soil and pollen and particles of mash for the cows and chickens and woolly chaff and chick feathers and cow hairs and tiny crumbs of dry cow and chicken dung, this massive army riding the wings of the wind and looking for a breach through which to penetrate and besoil.

Along with the increase in fast and heavy vehicles like tractors and cars came an increase in the dust, and Grandma Tonia began fighting with the drivers and even installed a sprinkler on the path next to our house. When it came to dust or mud, she preferred the latter. Mud was stickier and heavier and more obvious to the naked eye, whereas dust was slyer, more secretive, as well as more charming and light.

I remember that as a child I loved to watch the golden dancing of dust motes caught in morning rays of sunshine. Our bedroom in Jerusalem faced north, so I never saw them there. But the windows of the children's bedroom in our house in Nahalal faced east, and the room where I slept on visits to Grandma Tonia's faced northeast, so it was possible to see them shining like specks of gold in the first morning rays that breached the spaces between the slats of the shutters.

This was one of the most mesmerizing sights of my childhood and for me, contemplating these glimmers was a very pleasant way to start the day. As I have already recounted, I was obliged to get out of bed before sunrise when I stayed at Grandma Tonia's house, but on the Sabbath I was allowed to sleep later, and once, while I lay in bed contemplating the golden dancing of the dust motes, she came into my room and instead of pulling the mattress out from under me invited me to drink a cup of tea with her—and not outside on the porch, but in the kitchen. I, however, was caught up in my own world. "I'll come soon," I told her. "When they stop dancing."

"Dancing? When who'll stop dancing?" my grandmother asked, suspicious. She was always on guard—that someone would dirty the house on her, "runoff" from her, get married on her to someone with children from a previous marriage, leave stains or marks or scritch the walls on her. Now, suddenly, someone was dancing on her? This dance—who it belonged to or what it was, she did not know—was a bad omen.

I was young and naïve and had no idea what was about to happen. "Look, Grandma," I said, pointing at the air.

She looked and was alarmed. "Just yesterday I cleaned here and already the house is full of dust!"

The invitation was revoked, the chance of hearing a story over tea and a cookie had faded. "*Ah-nu,* up with you," she said. "Stop stinking up the bed, I need to clean, even though today is Shabbat."

22

In the days to follow another problem arose: at the time that the vacuum cleaner arrived in the village, the afternoon wind was blowing in the Jezreel Valley, so when Uncle Yitzhak gave the American rags to Grandma Tonia, all the American newspapers that had served as padding inside the box scattered. No one thought much about it, but several days later a few pages were found clinging to the branches of Grandpa Aharon's special citrus tree, the tree that in the meantime had produced corn, artichokes, and beans.

Grandpa Aharon hastened to pull them from there and, without thinking about it, glanced at the pages. He did not know English, but seeing the photographs and the advertisements was enough for him to understand the enormity of the danger. He appealed to the committee and at once a search team was organized and given the express instructions to find, gather, and destroy all these bits of newspaper before they could cause the damage they were liable to cause.

The job was not easy. The wind had carried the pages to all sorts of places. Some were found in the ditches beside the road or caught in the gutters running the length of the chicken coops. Some were discovered folded and hidden inside volumes of movement journals or farm magazines, or stuck and concealed in bales of hay in the barns. The danger was noted and dealt with in time. People, especially the younger generation, returned to their good reading habits, to the books in their homes and in the library, the *Davar* newspaper, the village bulletin.

Grandma Tonia knew nothing of this ruckus. First of all

because this sort of thing held no interest for her and did not bother her. And second, because she was busy with her new toy. Indeed, the gift given by the double traitor had served its purpose: avenger and cleanser. Grandpa Aharon was put out by the new American presence in his home but did not stand a chance against Grandma Tonia, who was happy and would clearly never agree to give up the sweeper she had received, or against the sweeper itself, which felt it had reached the place that every sweeper would be happy to be: in the home of a satisfied customer. The work was quite difficult and the local dust more coarse and problematic than the refined, filtered dust in America, but it managed quite successfully nonetheless. And as for this particular housewife, while pedantic, she still admired the sweeper's capability and actions.

However, as I hinted at earlier, beneath the surface impending disaster began to take shape and fate started smiling as it does each time it disrupts the plans of human beings, just before it bursts into its famous laughter. As always, this time as well there were early warnings. And as always, this time as well people had not learned to take heed, and certainly not right away. Grandma Tonia, naturally suspicious and quick-witted, felt these warnings but was bewitched by the magic of the vacuum cleaner.

It was only several nights later that she understood what had happened in her home, right under her nose. And on that night, in spite of her fatigue, she was unable to sleep. She rose from her bed, walked about the house, and in the end went to the sweeper, raised the cover she had spread over it—the reader may be unaware that dust dirties even vacuum cleaners—and stood gazing at it while the sweeper smiled obsequiously at its mistress, sparkling in the darkness. She gave it something between a caress and a cleaning swipe with her shoulder rag and returned to bed, still unable to sleep. For an entire hour she thought and thought until her feelings shaped themselves into words. She understood what it was that bothered her, a very simple question: Where was the dirt that her vacuum cleaner had sucked up? Where was the filth it had cleaned? With regular cleaning methods she could see the enemy passing through various stages of defeat and retreat: It was wiped away, washed away, swept away. It was collected and gathered on a dustpan, emptied into the waste bin, or taken to the cow muck. When she cleaned the floor, the dirt made the water in the bucket turn murky. When she dusted a piece of furniture, the dirt clung to the rag and was visible to the eye. But here, as with a magic wand, the moment the sweeper passed through a room all dirt disappeared from view, never to be seen again.

Her old friends and helpers—the broom, the rag, the brush, the dustpan, the rubbish bin, the cow muck—all did everything in plain view, for all to see, in a spirit of what we now call "transparency." But this was an act of wizardry—swipe, swipe, a little humming, some quiet growls, and suddenly everything was clean and smiling at her.

The mystery of it perturbed her. She had never before been in such close proximity to such a state-of-the-art appliance, so complex and inscrutable. Not that she turned her back on modernity or mistrusted it, heaven forbid. This was a woman who, in her youth, had drawn water from a Ukrainian well, while here in Palestine she had a house of her own with electricity and running water. Still, in the cowshed, the milker sat by the cow on the little stool known as a *taburetka* and milked with his hands, feeling the teat between his fingers and seeing the jet sprays of milk, their sound changing as the level of the white liquid rose in the pail. Corn was harvested with a scythe and alfalfa with a sickle or, at best, a horse-drawn reaping machine. They saw the heavy crops bend, they smelled the juice of the stalks as they turned the fingers green, and later they gathered and piled them with a pitchfork, feeling their full weight. In short, this American sweeper was carrying out an unfamiliar and inexplicable witchcraft that went against the laws of nature and common sense. It concealed dirt.

Grandma Tonia, as was mentioned, studied at a gymnasium and was able to recite whole pages of Russian poetry, but now, face-to-face with this mysterious American progress, felt like a Pacific Ocean islander when the first European ship appeared on its shores with its soaring masts and glorious sails and ingenious bow, and fired a shot from its cannon. There was a faraway explosion and a small cloud of smoke. No one understood what had happened, the cannonball was not even visible to the eye, and then a second later, on the beach, the village was aflame.

Where was the dirt disappearing to? She entertained and dismissed several alternatives, several of which frightened her so much that she could not even use words to describe them to herself. She was a very practical woman who had no use for mysticism but did have a healthy intuition for the law of conservation of mass, especially if the mass was dirt. Thus, it took her only a few hours of thinking and pondering and wandering from the general to the specific and back again to reach a clear conclusion: the dirt must be inside the sweeper itself! There was no other possibility. It would have to be opened and inspected.

She gave it a sidelong glance so that it would not discern her suspicions or her plans, because a creature like this, if it understood that it was under suspicion, might behave in an unexpected manner, vomiting all at once all the impurity in its guts and escaping at a clip to the fields. Perhaps that would even be preferable, for a vacuum cleaner resides inside the house, and the house was her very own, and thus it was that the hidden dirt was found inside her house. Out of sight, but nevertheless there it was, right inside her house. And dirt was dirt. Filth. Impurity.

Who knew what that dirt might have in store for her, crouching there deep inside that new vacuum cleaner and scheming.

Thus it was that she walked about finding no respite, her left cheek reddening with rage. And since she feared opening the sweeper and dismantling it—what would she find inside? How would she react? How would it react? And what if she damaged something? And how would she put it back together?—she summoned Yitzhak from Kfar Yehoshua.

Her brother came, heard her complaint, and burst out laughing.

"Of course it's inside the sweeper," he said. "Where did you think, Tonichka? It cleaned the whole house, collected the dirt, and now it needs to be opened and emptied."

"If there is dirt inside," Grandma Tonia said, "then it's dirty." And again, for emphasis: "It's dirty!" she said, as though casting blame or announcing Job's tidings to herself.

"It's not so bad, Tonichka," said Yitzhak. "It just means that every once in a while it needs to be cleaned, too, like you clean any other machine."

"Clean it, too?" she said, astonished. "I've cleaned the entire house. Now I have to clean it as well?" She grew angry. "So that means cleaning the same dirt twice! Why didn't anyone tell me this before?!"

Suddenly, she was furious not only with the vacuum cleaner, and with her husband, and with her brother-in-law, Uncle Yeshayahu, and with her brother, who kept calling her Tonichka instead of helping her, but also with the American woman on the outside of the box, that overdressed housewife she thought was her ally. Everyone had deceived her, each in his own way.

"It's a very modern appliance," he told her. "It not only cleans, it also collects the dirt. It is a rag and a broom and a dustpan and a rubbish bin all in one."

His voice took on an expansive tone as he raved about the sweeper. "It's a household combine, Tonichka. It reaps and threshes and winnows and gathers. But now it needs to be opened so the dirt inside can be removed and thrown away."

This soothing analogy in fact caused Grandma Tonia to become even more perturbed, because a combine does not make anything disappear. The wheat is winnowed to its separate parts and these are exposed for all the world to see: sack of seeds, clouds of chaff, and mounds of hay. Nothing on the outside is made to disappear and nothing is hidden on the inside. What's more, how could they be compared? Combines operate outside, in fields that are anyhow filled with dirt, while the sweeper is inside the house, inside her clean house.

"It's dirty," she said again. "Inside my house. An appliance filled with dirt."

"You can see it that way, Tonichka. But what's the harm? A rubbish bin is kept inside the house and it's filled with dirt, too."

"Your Haya keeps the rubbish bin inside," Grandma Tonia said, raising her voice. "In my house it's next to the porch, completely outside." Then she added, "And a rubbish bin is a rubbish bin! That's exactly what it's called: a rubbish bin! And here, in my house, right inside, there's an appliance that cleans, which is how the svieeperrr presents itself, and yet it's dirty!"

Yitzhak understood that his mistake was more fundamental and deeper than he had originally assumed, that theirs were two completely different worldviews. He realized that he should have explained how the machine worked right from the beginning, step by step, from the cleaning right through getting rid of the dirt. He should have insisted upon taking apart the sweeper and explaining how it worked before the first use.

He tried to do that now, but it was too late. When it came to anything having to do with dirt, his sister was highly suspicious. She knew the way it conducted itself, how it schemed, how it was vigilant and sneaky, how it concealed itself, slunk about, amassed, multiplied, pushed its way in through every crack, was borne on the wind, clung. It became apparent that the double traitor had yet another form of treachery: the vacuum cleaner he had sent was nothing more than a Trojan horse, and worse—a collaborator.

At this point I must clarify that use of the Trojan horse image is mine and not Grandma Tonia's. I suspect that in spite of her close acquaintance with a number of horses, both in Ukraine and in Palestine, and in spite of her gymnasium education, the Trojan horse was not part of her analogical lineup. Moreover, I am not certain she would even have liked the *Iliad* or the *Odyssey*. First of all, she would have had no use for twenty years of anxious waiting like Penelope. The moment that Ulysses chose to "runoff" for Troy she would have chased him down and brought him back home so Ulysses would never have met up with those "whoors" of his, Circe and Calypso. And then there was the matter of all the men wishing to wed Penelope. It would be inconceivable to her that so many men would desire a woman with a son from a first marriage.

And still, because she did not possess the technical abilities of her brother, Yitzhak, she demanded that he open the sweeper at that very moment, right away, so she could learn its secrets. Yitzhak was pleased to have the opportunity to dismantle it, to learn and reassemble. He wasted no time in pulling out his tools and getting to work, but she pushed him aside. "Not in the house!" she exclaimed. "On the platform, over an old newspaper!"

The three of them went outside: Grandma Tonia, enraged; Uncle Yitzhak, blissful; and the sweeper, dirty, its dishonor about to be exposed. Yitzhak warned his sister about what she was about to see, his clever, nimble fingers already playing with several fasteners and clips, and popping the sweeper open.

Inside there were all manner of fans and cylinders and straps and transmissions, and dust and dirt, and, in the middle—ugly, repulsive, and foul as the bloated carcass of a toad—there was a cloth sack, absolutely full.

"It's here, inside this," Yitzhak said.

"Open it," Tonia said. "I want to see."

"I don't think that's a good idea, Tonichka," Yitzhak told her. "Here inside is the dirt it collected. It needs to be thrown away. I really don't think we should look."

"Open it."

Uncle Yitzhak opened the sack and poured its loathsome contents onto the newspaper. Grandma Tonia examined them and even poked around with the tip of her finger. Inside the regular grayish dirt several dead insects could be seen, along with several others still crawling, dazed and battered. There were human hairs, small crumbs of food—someone had been eating inside the house in spite of the absolute prohibition—and while she was still considering who the culprit might be she discovered a shred of clipped fingernail as well. Someone had clipped his fingernails inside the house and let them fall to the floor! Grandma Tonia took it, determined to figure out whose it was. She would find the guilty party and take chunks out of him.

But then something terrible happened. A breeze suddenly kicked up, and in front of her very eyes the small pile of filth lifted into the air and blew away. She sent up a cry of despair: some, if not all, of that dirt would make it back into her house.

Yitzhak at once understood the significance of the matter. "That shouldn't happen," he said, trying to calm her down. "The sack is emptied straight into the rubbish bin and the rubbish is taken to the dump."

"Maybe it wasn't supposed to happen," Grandma Tonia said, "but it did. And now it also has to be gathered up all over again, and the svieeperrr itself needs to be cleaned."

From atop her shoulder she removed her loyal rag, the only family member she could rely on, and sighed. *"Ah-nu,* see for yourself, Yitzhak, what it looks like. It's not only what was inside the sack but also all around. The svieeperrr itself is dirty. I need to clean it. Look how much dirt and dust there is here. And here. And here, too."

Indeed, specks of dust could even be spotted on the sweeper's inner parts, as well as a few bits of scum.

"That's its life, Tonichka," Yitzhak said with a smile. "Tractors get dirty from mud and grease. Brushes get dirty from paint. The sickle gets rusty from the alfalfa. Fishmongers smell of fish and vacuum cleaners get dirty from dust."

"I need to clean it," Grandma Tonia repeated. Yitzhak could hear the disappointment and desperation in her voice. She asked him to break down the machine further, into smaller parts. This meant using a range of screwdrivers and wrenches of every kind, which brought him great pleasure.

He dismantled the sweeper and laid out its parts according to the order in which he had removed them atop a big old sheet his sister spread out for him on the platform before she cleaned each and every part in the old way—first with wet, then soap, again with wet, finish with dry—and not with some gadget or system suited to Americans or traitors who had become Americans. She cleaned them, covered them, and asked Yitzhak to reassemble it all.

"If that's what you're going to do after every use of the sweeper," he said, "then it really is redundant. It's supposed to help you, not make your life more difficult. And I can't come here twice a week to take it apart and put it together each time. I'll find you a buyer for it. I have a rich friend, a contractor from Haifa. He'll be happy to buy it for his wife."

But Grandma Tonia never gave up on anything. Not her farm, not her land, not the cleaning of her house, not her husband. Nobody was going to inherit her as long as she was alive. She announced that "the svieeperrr stays here!"

And then something else happened, the ramifications of which would only be understood many years later. Yitzhak was continuing to put the sweeper back together, examining and learning each part of it, when suddenly he came upon a sealing ring that caused him to sit up straight and say, "Tonichka, I'm afraid there's something wrong with this sealing ring."

"Something wrong?" she said, alarmed. "What now?"

"Don't worry. It's fine for the moment and will continue to be fine for a long, long time, and maybe it'll never be a problem. But one day, years from now, this sealing ring may lose its sealing power and some dust could escape."

"Some dust? Escape? Where?"

"I'm not sure it will even escape, and if it did it would only be a little bit."

Grandma Tonia stood up. The decision to imprison this traitorous sweeper and never use it again was formed at that very moment.

When Yitzhak finished the reassembling she grabbed hold of the tube and went to the second door, the sweeper following along in silent obedience, unaware what fate awaited it. She entered the house, passed through the dining room, and turned toward the forbidden bathroom. The sweeper rolled along behind her, curious and excited to know what it would be vacuuming in there, when suddenly the cloth sack in which it had arrived was thrust upon it and two strong hands lifted it and placed it inside the box, and the sturdy white rope that Uncle Yeshayahu had used was tied tight around it and then it was forced into a straitjacket in the form of an old sheet, brother of those that covered the furniture in the locked rooms, and atop that, a blanket, after which its mistress left the bathroom and closed the door behind her.

Darkness, like in the belly of the ship and the train carriages. Silence. The sound of a key being inserted and turned. The door was locked.

23

In the year 1935 or 1936, when my grandmother's vacuum cleaner was assembled at one of the General Electric factories in the United States, it never could have imagined the journeys, adventures, and reversals of fortune that lay ahead in its future. It certainly could not have imagined what actually happened next. It probably thought its life would pass much like the lives of its peers from the assembly line: from the gates of the factory to the distribution warehouses and from there, after a short waiting period, a trip to a shop, where it would wait in its box in a storeroom, or be presented to customers in a tantalizing way on the showroom floor or even the shop window, where it would wait to be sold, then brought to some home, where it would meet its owners and begin to work.

The life of the average vacuum cleaner passes in a monotonous fashion. It is operated once or twice a week by the same person—sometimes a man, but usually a woman—and, like them, lives a drab life passing through the same rooms over and over and vacuuming up the same particles. Only occasionally would it know some small excitement: a crumb of unknown extraction, an unfamiliar hair, or even something really big— today the sack is being emptied! And even—what a surprise—a new carpet has been purchased!

Sometimes a naughty child will experiment with it: Can a dog be vacuumed? Can it catch a paper airplane in flight, or a hapless cockroach as it scurries to its hideaway under the sink? It happens that couples split up and then the vacuum cleaner usually stays with her, the husband disappearing from its life and finding a new woman with a vacuum cleaner of her own that remained with her when she split up from her own husband.

My grandmother's sweeper merited a far more fascinating life. First of all, it did not make the standard, ordinary trip from factory to store and from there to the home of someone in the very neighborhood; instead, it took an exceedingly long journey over seas and continents, waves and mountains, roads and railroad tracks, and, finally, a farmer's wagon hitched to a white horse, blue eyes, the yellow of a pencil and corn stubble, a green field.

It enjoyed it all, even felt a sort of pride. But now, in the darkness of the bathroom, it understood that sometimes a standard, ordinary life is preferable, like the lives of all other people and vacuum cleaners. Why hadn't it stayed in America? it asked itself. Why wasn't it sent to some normal American housewife in a polka-dot dress with red lips and manicured nails? A woman as American as it was, someone who understands how the American way of cleaning works. So what—it wouldn't get dirty? Of course it would get dirty! That is precisely its job. It toils and gets soiled so that she may enjoy a clean house, pampered hands, and a smiling face.

And that is not all: on its journey to Palestine the vacuum cleaner had at least the illusion that it knew what lay ahead, that it was bound for a housewife who awaited its arrival so that it might clean her house; whereas now, imprisoned in the bathroom, uncertainty and suspicion gnawed away at it, followed by desperation, and, finally, understanding and insight. The sweeper understood that it would never again see the light of day.

Along with it in the bathroom were several other of

Grandma Tonia's prisoners: three pristine china services, elegant tablecloths with lace edges that had never been spread on a table, brand-new bed linens never slept on or dreamed on or made love on. But no other inmate had sinned as it had and been condemned to a life sentence.

On the outside, life continued. Trees produced fruit. Chickens laid eggs. Cows oozed milk. Herring was prepared and eaten. Walls and floors were washed, wet and dry, with soap and with kerosene. Mud stuck to shoes, filth to fingertips. Dust flew through the air, trying to get in and succeeding at the neighbors', but at Grandma Tonia's it was repelled.

Time passed. Grandchildren were born and grew up. They bathed in the trough at the edge of the pavement, heard stories from their parents: Here is the special citrus tree that grandfather planted; today it bears plain old grapefruit but once it bore anchovies and tomatoes. Here there once slithered a viper that I killed with a broom. A shoe brush? Who told you a story like that? Here is where we tethered our intelligent jennet, Ah, who spent nights flying to visit kings and palaces. Where did she most love to visit? Where lived the king who gave her the largest portion of grain.

And there were insults as well. Far away from there, in America, Uncle Yeshayahu was even more offended than when the dollars he had sent were mailed back to him. The rumors that reached him this time were that Grandma Tonia—whom he had expected to play the role of ally—despised his gift and would not use it, and this hurt him. He knew that the pioneers in Palestine were revolutionaries and, as is the way of revolutionaries, could be extreme and uncompromising. And as a proud and knowledgeable American he knew that these were Socialists, which is to say dangerous people. But now he understood that Grandma Tonia, in her own way, was an idealist of

157

even bigger and harsher convictions and, where he was concerned, immeasurably more dangerous.

Years passed, memories settled and were invented, stories were told and sprouted different versions, and all the while the American sweeper sat in a locked bathroom in Nahalal. Each time we visited Grandma Tonia and were permitted to enter the house and draw near the locked doors of the forbidden rooms my mother would repeat what she always said: "Behind this door is my mother's furniture." And in front of the bathroom door, "And behind this one is her sweeper."

The air stood still. The few motes of dust in the bathroom sank to the floor. Voices could be heard on the other side of the door: furniture being moved, water mopped up with a wrung rag, the loud ticking of the alarm clock, Grandma Tonia and Grandpa Aharon quarreling, his dwindling poems, her increasing complaints, the barn owl outside and the nighttime snoring in response—hers thin and curling, his louder and louder, frightening themselves, stopping, then starting all over again.

A year and then another and another. For forty years the sweeper lived in dark and lonely confinement wrapped in its white shroud and as clean as the day it was born, untainted by dust. Its hinges were still; its fan was silenced; its thick tube lay motionless as a snake carcass. My mother told me that on occasion her mother would open that door. A sliver of light and hope would suddenly expand there; there was a quick glance, a counting of the prisoners to make sure there were no "runoffs," a check for dust—had some grain of dirt managed to penetrate the locked door?—and at once the door was closed again. Darkness and silence, forty years. Few prisoners have been incarcerated for so extended a period and without respite. I do not know how a vacuum cleaner feels the passing of time, but forty years is forty years. A long time.

And then, one day, or, more precisely, one night, the sweeper thought it was hearing the language that it heard back there, before it arrived here, so many long years earlier. On the other side of the wall were words and the accent that were its own, and they belonged to a woman. A young woman. Someone from its homeland.

Several hours later, the door was opened, a switch clicked, and a light went on. Grandma Tonia unknotted the white rope that had come with it on its journey to Palestine, removed the blanket and the old sheet, pulled it up and out of the box, and slipped the sack off it. The vacuum cleaner looked at her and was astonished. Forty years had passed. It and the American woman in the picture on the box remained as young as they had been, while she was so old that it scarcely recognized her. Only the rag on her shoulder looked familiar, even though it had been through seven hundred wash cycles. It was one of the excellent American rags that had traveled with the sweeper, back then.

Grandma Tonia passed this rag down the shininess of its body, caught sight of her own twisted reflection in its curves, took hold of its large, thick tube, and pulled it gently.

Once again the sweeper was following its mistress. Its silent wheels did not make a sound. She turned and walked with it out of the bathroom.

24

From the time I turned thirteen and until I was enlisted in the army I came to Nahalal during school holidays and summer vacations in order to work on the farm and help my uncles with whatever needed doing.

As a youth I was a much more industrious worker than I was as a child. I no longer looked for ways to get out of working or offered to tell stories to those doing the real labor, especially since the stories told by Menahem and Yair were far more interesting than my own. They taught me all the farmwork, including milking (by hand and by machine); the feeding of newborn calves; cleaning the cowshed; harvesting and gathering; milking semen from male turkeys and inseminating the females—two loathsome jobs, the details of which I will spare you; egg gathering and cleaning with my aunts; and the most desirable job of all, driving the tractor and operating the machines and agricultural instruments connected to it; but also the skill that turns any old farmer's son into a person of merit—driving a wagon with a plowshare in reverse, and more than that, backing up a wagon that has a plowshaft.

I started with the easier tasks, like cleaning the troughs and laying irrigation lines. After that I learned to hitch Whitey to the wagon and, each morning, when the uncles were getting ready for the milking, he and I were sent to bring mangold-wurzel for the cows. Mangold-wurzel is a root vegetable with very thick roots and is closely related to sugar beets, which please the palates of cows to no end.

We would set out from the yard, pass by the vineyard that was uprooted several years later, and skirt the edge of the citrus grove that would be felled in the future. It was early in the morning and the air was still cool and fragile, dew clinging to the grapefruit leaves. The drops that fell to the ground were immediately swallowed up and made a surprisingly loud rustling sound, almost a crack, when they hit a dried leaf.

The earth heated with the pace of the horse. The sun rolled back the fog that swaddled the fields. A flock of early-rising goldfinches suddenly swirled into a delirious cloud of color. Today

I no longer see the goldfinches; they have been hunted to near extinction and have disappeared like the large flocks of starlings that covered the eye of heaven back then as a billowing cloth, and—like the song thrushes, which I heard and saw every day as they cracked open snails on the pavement, and the rufous bush robins, their rust-colored tails beckoning to me from the eucalyptus grove of Nahalal, which also exists no longer—have been uprooted from the ground but not from memory.

The turnip patch grew at the bottom of our parcel—which is what each family's land is called on a moshav—by the abandoned British antiaircraft post once used to guard the nearby military airstrip. Whitey, placable and good-natured, had grown old. He seemed to have forgotten the wedding day of Penina and Menahem, when I hurled eggs at him in the shed, and even if he had not forgotten, he had forgiven me. He walked slowly, sensing that the hands holding the reins were not as experienced or as decisive as those of Menahem and Yair, but he did not exploit this fact. He was quite familiar with the division of labor between us. At first it was easy for us both, a gentle ride down to the field with an empty cart. Next, at the field, came the hard part for me, the picking of the heavy turnips and piling them onto the cart. After that came the hard part for him, pulling the full cart back to our yard, and then it was my turn to toil again, tossing the turnips into the cow pen.

It was in those days that Menahem and Yair bought their first tractor, a little Ferguson on which I learned to drive and work. The Ferguson was not capricious, was faster and stronger than Whitey, and was not in the habit of running away at night on the prowl for female tractors. In short order, the aging horse found himself unemployed, replaced in most of his tasks—a fact that did not, heaven forbid, fill him with sorrow—and in the end my uncles decided to put him out to pasture. He spent his last two years of life in the cow pen, near their trough, where he pestered them with his stories about life during the British Mandate.

During that period I grew apart from Grandma Tonia a bit. I was no longer a little boy but an adolescent, and I enjoyed the company of kids my age, as well as that of my uncle Yair, more than I enjoyed spending time with her. Once I even had a little argument with her over her German beer stein. I asked once again if I could have it, and once again she said, "You're not going to inherit me as long as I'm alive!" The truth is, however, that even before that our relationship had had its ups and downs. We never had a real fight—an achievement in and of itself when it came to my grandmother—but more than once I heard people saying unpleasant things about her and sometimes I felt the same embarrassment that a child is liable to feel when a family member is being spoken ill of, just as my mother herself had felt it. It was worse now that I was growing up, and Grandma Tonia's complaints and habits aroused a malaise in me, and impatience. But after I had grown up yet a little bit more I found a new and good trait in her, one that made us coconspirators. It turned out that she was liberal and open-minded when it came to matters of guys and girls, more so than any other member of the family.

Later, my mother told me that she had always been that way, that she and her sister, Batsheva, had been the only two girls in the village who were given sex education by their mother, with explanations about menstruation and other matters that in that generation were not discussed, and which fell upon their friends without warning. As for me, I discovered that I could bring a girlfriend to Grandma Tonia's and be given a room and a *mishkav* without a hitch, without her grimacing or poking around with nosy questions. She would even smile and say, "Enjoy yourselves!" instead of "Good night" before bed.

Furthermore, on one occasion that I took advantage of her

hospitality, Grandma Tonia looked at my girlfriend, pulled me aside under some pretext, and said quietly but with a note of criticism in her voice, "That's the same girl you brought here last time."

"She's my girlfriend, Grandma. You don't like her?"

She said, "Never mind if I like her. I want you to bring a different girl each time you come to visit."

When she saw the astonishment on my face, she added, "You're a young man. A young man should change girls like he does socks." In case anyone is in doubt, or thinks I have taken undue literary liberties, I will state that this is an exact quote, exactly what she said.

"So maybe that's why you sent her to bathe in your 'excellent shower' in the cowshed," I said. "That way she won't agree to come back here with me a second time."

Grandma Tonia ignored this comment. She added, "And you'll always get a room here with a bed, and you won't have to go rolling around in the fields."

Grandma Tonia on her way to the "excellent shower" in the cowshed, early 1930s

I grew apart from Grandpa Aharon, too, though even before that I was not as close to him as I was to her. He had grown old, inward, and secretive, was working on writing his memoirs. Afternoons he spent napping under one of the trees or reading a book or an old newspaper, and from time to time he would rouse himself to work on one of the jobs he found for himself: collecting leftover pieces of metal wire ("wire-pieces") and rope; shaking out and folding old feed sacks; gathering wood planks, which he called "plinks." Aside from keeping him gainfully employed, this work expressed the spirit of the moshav movement perfectly: Nothing is ever thrown away. Everything has its purpose and its need and its reason. It can be recycled, used for fertilizer or feeding, or a thousand other uses.

This was especially true for "wire-pieces." Like all moshavniks, Grandpa Aharon picked them up from the ground and tucked them into his pockets for a simple reason: a little wire-piece like this could get into the trough and a cow could swallow it. And anyway, a little wire-piece is a farmer's best friend. You can use it to hold together a tear in a horse's harness, secure the door of the chicken coop, mend the fence, unplug a clogged sprinkler. Our family storytellers even awarded its miraculous properties a place of honor: Uncle Arik, Aunt Batsheva's husband, gave his tractor an overhaul with a wire-piece and Ah, our clever jennet, used one to pick the lock of the cowshed, race into the yard, flap its ears, and soar up and away to visit the Russian czar in Moscow. When Ah was born there were no longer czars in Russia? Never mind.

25

My story is nearing its conclusion and, in my humble opinion, its climax as well. And since this part I did not hear from my mother or from any other person, but rather was witness to it and even took part in it myself, it is clear to me that this is how it was, the absolute truth. But before I get to it I must first tell the other version of how my grandmother's sweeper reached the village. I recount it here for the sole purpose of being fair, so that no one will be insulted and so that I will not find myself in trouble with still more relatives than the ones I have already angered.

And so, this is how it was: Several years after the establishment of the State of Israel, in the early 1950s, Uncle Yeshayahu came to visit the family in Israel. He had a sister and a brother there whom he had not seen in more than forty years, and those siblings had sons and daughters and grandsons and granddaughters he had never met, and in spite of everything we thought about him and said about him with regard to his double treachery, the establishment of the State of Israel caused him great joy and excitement.

Uncle Yeshayahu's main purpose for the trip was to make peace with his brother Aharon, but he also wished to impress the family, to show everyone that he, too, had achievements and successes. And while he had not drained the swamps or founded a moshav or a nation, he did not arrive in Israel empty-handed. He brought many gifts, both large and small, which attested to his affluence and his generosity and were meant to pave the way to his return to the family.

. . .

In honor of his visit, the family gathered in Herzliya at the home of Aunt Sarah, sister of Uncle Yeshayahu and Grandpa Aharon. This was an emotional gathering for all; it does not happen every day that a family experiences such a coming together, but it must be said that the gifts certainly added to the excitement. And indeed, Uncle Yeshayahu splurged on everyone and did not leave out a soul. He brought delicacies unavailable in Israel at the time, during the days of austerity: salami and instant coffee and fruit preserves and chocolate bars and tubes of condensed milk; he brought bed linens and clothing and toys and all sorts of other luxuries that Grandpa Aharon scrutinized with a critical eye but did not say a word about so as to avoid another rift.

But there were larger gifts as well, truly large, and these arrived separately. Like Jacob of the Bible, who sent herds of sheep and cattle to his brother Esau in order to appease him before arriving, so too did Uncle Yeshayahu send several enormous wooden crates ahead of himself, and these contained presents for his sister, his brother, his sister-in-law, and his nieces and nephews. He was especially generous toward Grandma Tonia because he wished to make up with her husband. In a large crate that arrived at Haifa port there was a Frigidaire—the refrigerator from which Grandma would remove the cream she put in my mouth each time I came for a visit looking "vorn down." And since he knew she did the laundry in a large basin heated in early times over a bonfire and now—the height of technology at the time—over a Primus stove, he had tossed in an Easy brand washing machine and spin dryer, an American giant that stood on three legs and held two drums, one with an "agitator" for the laundry and the other with a "centrafuga," as Grandma called it, for wringing.

A sweeper arrived then, too—not large, not shiny, not General Electric, no big, silent wheels or attachment heads—just a plain Electrolux vacuum cleaner, small and dull and wheelless, its body covered in gray vinyl.

In short, there was no wooden crate beautifully packed, no American sea captain with gold-barred sleeves, no French captain as tall as a mast, no fast continental trains or slow Jezreel Valley trains, no white horse, green field, red polka-dot dress. None of it! Just a small, modest sweeper brought to Israel by Uncle Yeshayahu, and not in the 1930s but after the War of 1948.

This lifeless version is unacceptable as far as I am concerned. First of all because it was not the first time I had heard the truth contested by other versions of various family stories. And second because I side with an established rule whose roots can be found not in law or literature but in the world of science: researchers say that if a certain phenomenon has several plausible explanations then the most simple of them should be adopted. Similarly, if a certain story has several versions that sound correct, in our family we adopt the most beautiful of them. And what could be more beautiful than the sweeper's aliyah to Israel in a wooden crate containing a box with a picture of a winsome and smiling woman standing on her head like a scallion, and the field, and the cart, and the blue and the yellow, and all of this exposed to the astonished eyes of the entire village? Certainly not a tiresome day spent in the customs office of Haifa port.

Most important of all, however, is the fact that one night, many years later, I saw the vacuum cleaner with my very own eyes. And it was a General Electric, its year of production correct according to my mother's version of events, and it had large, silent wheels and was even bigger and flashier than in her tale.

26

This is how it was: One day, when I was a young university student in Jerusalem, I entered the post office located in the Mahane Yehuda market, for the purpose of sending two books to a girlfriend of mine who was working in a hospital in the United States. We had met and become friends some two years earlier when she was a nurse at HaEmeq Hospital in Afula and I was a patient for several months after being wounded during my army service.

Ahead of me in line stood a suntanned girl in a white cotton shirt, short pants, and sandals. She was different from the other people waiting in line. It was obvious that she was not from Mahane Yehuda, or Jerusalem, or even Israel for that matter. True, she was wearing biblical sandals, but they were brand-new, and the strap on one of them had already raised a small and touching blister on her heel. The clip holding a long curl of hair above the nape of her neck was quite special. Her shorts were indeed men's shorts, but not the Israeli blue ATA shorts, with pockets that hung below the hem, that everyone wore in those days; hers were greenish safari shorts from abroad, with square, tailored pockets. Today young Westerners from around the world have a similar look and wear similar clothing, often appearing to be wearing a uniform, but back then there was variety and individual character.

She even exuded a different scent, which I remember well. My sense of smell is good and I remember smells; the scent of this girl seemed to be a mixture of seawater and the large, orange peaches that I think were called Somerset but can no longer be found in the Mahane Yehuda market or in any other market, and these, too, I miss terribly.

I could not see her face but her backside was quite pleasant to look at. She had a sculptured neck and firm legs, and on the floor in front of her was a package with writing in English. Each time the line advanced she would push it ahead with her sandaled foot in a lazy motion that was completely enchanting.

She seemed to sense my presence behind her, perhaps because of my efforts at reading what was written on her package, because suddenly she turned around and stared at me. I was happy to discover that she, like me, wore glasses. We exchanged the small smiles of the nearsighted. I said, "Shalom." In American English she said, "I'm a tourist," and added in American Hebrew, "I don't speak Hebrew." She turned back around.

The line moved slowly. I had enough time to envy the package at her feet, to peruse the top vertebrae of her spine, which stood out from her nape, and to imagine their sister vertebrae down below, one by one, in her neck, her chest, her waist, all the way down to the sacrum and the tailbone, those small evolutionary leftovers that disappear into the flesh and are immovable. Anatomy and evolution experts say that the role they play is not at all clear, but to me, at that moment, it was absolutely clear.

I was suddenly overcome with sadness, sorry that I was not among those men who possess the daring and the capability to initiate small talk. But luck was in my favor, and when the young woman reached the counter, my chance arose. The small, mustachioed postal clerk did not know English and the girl, as she had let me know earlier, did not know Hebrew. She turned to me once again and asked if I could help her translate.

I assisted her in sending the package, and when she was finished she left the post office—and I accompanied her.

She laughed. "You forgot to send your package," she said.

I was embarrassed. "I'll send it another time, it's not urgent."

"Go back in and send it," she said. "I'll wait here for you."

She stood in the shade of a stone wall while I went back inside the post office. After the usual Israeli arguments—"I was here before" and "Ask him, ask this guy, he saw me"—I sent my packet of books and hastened to leave, praying she would still be there, that she would not have left.

"That's it," I said. "I sent it."

"To whom?" she asked.

"A friend," I said. "She's in the United States."

"What's she doing there?"

"She's a nurse," I told her. "She's working at a hospital in Los Angeles. And who was your package for?"

"My boyfriend. He's in Los Angeles, too."

"Great," I said. "So our packages will travel together all the way there from the Mahane Yehuda market."

"And maybe my boyfriend and your girlfriend will meet at the Los Angeles post office," she said. "And he'll help her pick up her package like you helped me."

I told her that was a very likely scenario, and although nothing was stated explicitly, it was clear to us both that we needed to preempt the possibility of an inappropriate meeting in Los Angeles between her boyfriend and my girlfriend with our own, right here and now.

She asked if I knew anywhere cheap she could eat, and since we were at the edge of the market I grew daring and asked if she would like to eat together at one of the kebab places on Agrippas Street. It was in those days that that most authentic and greasy dish called Jerusalem mixed grill was invented, and Abigail—who had just introduced herself—said she would be happy to try one.

When she said her name, Abigail—Abigail, not the Hebrew Avigayil—she extended her hand and shook mine boldly, which pleased me just as much as the way she had pushed that box with her foot and as much as her straightforward way of speaking. We went to the restaurant; we ate and chatted. Her face was expressive and full of humor and it had a characteristic that I love in human beings, male and female: it beamed.

She told me she was doing a master's degree in special education, she was twenty-five years old, born in Chicago, and as a girl had moved to Los Angeles with her family. The boyfriend to whom she had sent the package was also studying special education, and they were due to be married the following summer. I told her I was also a college student, twenty-two years old, and that I was working nights as an ambulance driver for Magen David Adom, the Israeli Red Cross, and during the day I raised white mice at the psychology lab of the Hebrew University, and apparently I, too, would wed one day, but not to the girlfriend to whom I had sent my package.

I asked her where in Jerusalem she was living and she told me that she had a room at one of the hostels in the Old City. She had arrived in Israel only a week earlier and had been to Tel Aviv; now she wished to travel to Galilee. Once again I dared to make an offer, this time to travel together. She said yes. "But to where and how?" she asked. I told her we would take the bus and we could sleep at my grandmother's house in a village in the Jezreel Valley. After that we would see. I told her I had a lot of friends up north.

"We'll sleep at your grandmother's?" she asked, flabbergasted. "Your grandmother's?!" She laughed. "I've never met a guy who invited me to have a good time at his grandmother's house before."

"Abigail," I said, "I don't know any of the guys you've been out with until now, but when it comes to grandmothers, I'm willing to compete with them all. My grandmother is an unusual one, and she'll be very happy to see that I've come with a girl."

I knew what I was talking about. My grandmother, in spite of all her quirks, and perhaps because of them, had a very special personality. And when she cared to, she could be interesting and even charming, in her own strange way. She had aged quite a bit, of course, but she had not lost her ability to tell stories, and on a good day she could fascinate and enchant any girl I brought to visit—all but one, whom she handed a bucket and a rag and told to start cleaning.

"Even without me," I told Abigail, "it would be worth your while just to meet my grandmother."

We planned to meet two and a half hours later at the central bus station. I raced off to Magen David Adom in order to switch shifts, then to the university to take my leave of the mice and my rented room, where I packed a bag. We met by the central bus ticket office, traveled to Haifa, and then switched to an all-stops bus bound for Afula. We talked the entire way, and on the ascent toward Tivon she asked that we swap glasses—"just for a moment"—to see how we saw each other and how we looked to each other.

It was a sweet and exciting moment of resemblance and difference, of testing and trusting, a sort of first kiss that grew misty, then focused, and preceded the real ones to come. Any couple that wears glasses will know what I mean, and whoever does not, well, there is no point in wasting words on uncomprehending eyes. Either way, it was clear at that moment that Abigail, too, would like the sleeping arrangements at Grandma Tonia's.

We got off the bus at the Nahalal junction and continued on foot into the village. The pleasant and familiar smell of straw, casuarina trees, and dust filled the air. A farmer on a tractor stopped to offer us a ride. We sat close together in his wagon, our shoulders touching and our arms lengthening the touch to our elbows. Her skin was blessed not only with the pleasant scent of peaches and the sea but also with a particularly silky touch. Our faces drew closer and we kissed for the first time. It was a smiling, bespectacled, short, and modest kiss. The farmer and his tractor did not feel a thing.

From the center of the village we walked to Grandma Tonia's house. Only then did I explain to Abigail what awaited her there.

"It's not the simplest matter to be hosted at my grandmother's house," I said.

"What's her problem?"

"She's got a dirt phobia," I said.

"No problem," she said. "My mother does, too."

I smiled politely. "Abigail," I said, "I think you don't understand what I'm saying, about what level of cleaning we're talking about."

"My mother," she said, "cleans between the kitchen tiles with toothpicks. She does that herself because she doesn't trust the maid to do it."

"Abigail," I said, "you're getting warmer, but your mother is still in second place, and by a good margin. My grandmother washes walls, and she puts a small rag on every handle of every door and window so that dirty fingerprints won't touch them."

Abigail said, "My mother disinfects the shower after every use."

I burst out laughing. "At your house people actually shower in the shower? At my grandmother's, that's forbidden. We have a hose in the wall of the cowshed and that's an 'excellent shower,' if you don't mind my saying so."

"My mother," she said, "is still driving a 1950s Buick, but she replaces her vacuum cleaner every year, because maybe the new model cleans better and will suck in three more particles of dust from the carpet."

"Abigail," I said, "because of the compassion and affection I feel for you I did not want to bring up the subject of vacuum cleaners. But since you yourself brought it up, you should know that my grandmother, too, has a vacuum cleaner."

"So?" Abigail said, surprised—meaning, what's the big deal? Lots of people have vacuum cleaners. You don't need to be cleaning-crazy for that.

"She has a vacuum cleaner but she doesn't use it," I explained.

"Because it doesn't do the job well enough for her standards?"

"Worse. She doesn't use it because it gets dirty when it's used."

"What?!"

"That's right. It fills with dust and dirt and then it needs to be cleaned."

"You win," she said.

"As for the 'excellent shower' in the cowshed," I said, "you're going to shower in it this evening. All the cows will peek at you, and I will, too."

27

As the sun began to set we arrived at my grandmother's. I explained to Abigail that one did not enter the house via the front door. We went around back, to the second door. I explained to her that one did not step off the pavement onto the earth so as not to track dirt into the house. At the second door I explained to her that one did not open the door and enter. "Grandma . . . Grandma . . ." I called to her from outside.

She stepped outside and her face lit up. "How good that you're here," she said, her eyes checking out the new girlfriend

I had brought with me. I kissed both her cheeks and she was happy. I was no longer an adolescent boy and we had grown closer again. We sat on the porch. At once she discerned that I was looking "vorn down," but she said she had no cream to fill my mouth with and began to complain about Menahem, who had argued with her about something and had not separated cream for her at the dairy. She continued with other complaints: Grandpa had "runoff" to Binya and had been there for several days already; Yair had gone off to Haifa without telling her even though he knew she needed him to bring her some things from the city; Batsheva did not visit often enough while Batya, my mother, had visited Itamar at Hanita.

"Grandma," I said, "I did what you told me. I brought a new girlfriend, and you haven't even asked her name. Let me introduce you. Her name is Abigail, she is from America, she doesn't speak Hebrew, and our family troubles don't interest her."

"From America . . ." my grandmother said, impressed. She sighed and rose from her chair. I noticed she was limping and that her strong little body had started to weaken.

"Let's eat dinner and talk a little," she said. "After that I'll prepare the *mishkav* for the two of you."

Abigail, who was unaware of the layers of meaning in this ravishing Hebrew word for "bed," nevertheless understood the meaning of my grandmother's rise to her feet and said, "I'll help you," and stood up as well.

"No, please, sit," my grandmother said, using three of the nine words she knew in English, most of which she recalled from the days when British soldiers would come from the military airfield and, in defiance of the movement's constitution, bought some of her wonderful cheese. Incidentally, the other six words were "one," "two," "three," "stop," "svieeperrr," and "yes."

She turned to me and said, "Translate for me. Tell her I don't need help."

175

"She doesn't need help at the moment," I told Abigail, "but if she likes you then tomorrow you can help her clean."

Grandma Tonia prepared a simple and wonderful supper for us: a bowl filled with chilled slices of boiled potatoes, quartered hard-boiled eggs, slivers of radish and onion, and a light, tart sauce over all of it. On another plate there were chopped cucumbers and tomatoes. She cut bread for us, clutching the loaf to her breast, and from the refrigerator she removed the jewel in the crown: her pickled herring, swimming in oil, with allspice and a drop of vinegar and topped with many rings of onion and two bay leaves.

Her small body moved back and forth between the table and the stove, and I could see and hear that every limb and organ in it was contorted, painful, and groaning. Her fingers, from so much wringing, scouring, and milking. Her legs, from so much chasing after her husband and a decent living. Her back, from age and from carrying the weight of time and hard labor. But in spite of her frailty and the aching joints she complained about, she was in a good mood.

"That man," she told Abigail as she got the food on the table, "his nice grandfather, who everyone pities, makes a runoff each time to a convalescent home somewhere or to work, while the burden of the farm falls on my own two shoulders. Now tell her in English everything I just said."

I translated all this talk about my grandfather for Abigail, and she smiled. I was not surprised. It was clear to me from the start that there is no more efficient way of courting a girl than introducing her to my mother or my grandmother, who charmed them, each in her own way.

"Grandma," I said, "thank you for the meal. It's delicious."

"If your uncles had separated the cream for me then you and

your guest would have looked even healthier by now," she said. "But I see the herring helps. And the girl, too."

She said, "Tell her what you said to me, and explain to her that usually you don't give me compliments on my food."

"That's because you don't usually give me such good food," I said. "This time it seems I've brought someone you really like and you've decided to put yourself out for her."

The truth is that Grandma Tonia had served her two flagship dishes, as she was a very mediocre cook. She made a decent roast, and her plum jam and plum cake, which I have already mentioned, were excellent. But her best dishes needed no real cooking, and their biggest advantage was that they could be prepared outside the kitchen, without dirtying the stove and the countertop. One was the white bread she baked at Passover, and the other, the herring with boiled potatoes and hard-boiled eggs and radish and onion that she had served Abigail and me.

In general in our family, no one misses the cooking of any grandmother, even that grandmotherly classic known as chicken soup. My mother's chicken soup was better than her mother's chicken soup, and my sister's chicken soup and my own are better than our mother's, but preparing Grandma Tonia's chicken soup was an exciting experience, because it began with a command: "Go to the yard and fetch me . . ." and here she would note the color or name of one of the chickens.

The neighbors, she informed me, only made chicken soup according to the moshavniks' maxim: "When the moshavnik is ill or the chicken is ill." But not Grandma Tonia. She monitored the laying of eggs in her yard and knew who was laying more and who was laying less. A chicken who laid too few eggs was termed "a chicken not trying hard enough," and if she continued this sort of disobedience and sloth she would find herself on the family Sabbath table.

The chickens lived in the yard and laid eggs in wooden crates that Grandpa Aharon had padded with straw. There were a few geese as well, larger and heavier than I was as a child, and very aggressive. As geese are wont to do, they chased after me, their necks thrust forward and their wings stretched backward as a threat, and they tried to nip me with their flat and toothy beaks, which made every walk to the cowshed a frightening adventure.

I was not a particularly athletic child and the chickens ran much faster than I, but Grandma Tonia provided me with a long, thin metal pole with a hook at the end with which she taught me to catch the feet of the condemned chicken. Despite the fact that they are considered extremely stupid, they grasped the connection between this pole and what came next, so the moment they spied us in the yard they ran off in wild abandon, in every direction.

Filthy, fervid, and perspiring, I managed, finally, to catch the chicken who had not tried hard enough. I carried her by her ankles, upside down and squalling, while she, in a desperate attempt to save her life, raised her head and tried to peck my hands. I, however, had learned to hold her neck, shouting to Grandma Tonia to come quickly, that I had caught her. Grandma took her from me, produced a shaving blade, and slashed her throat.

This was a gruesome scene, riveting and repulsive at the same time. Grandma dropped the slaughtered chicken to the ground and it would run about the yard, blood spurting from its neck, until it collapsed, convulsed a bit more, shuddered one last shudder, and fell silent, when the plucking and dissection and cooking could begin. On Shabbat we ate the soup she had prepared, but, as I said, no one really misses it.

In short, while we do not miss the cooking of the previous generations, I do miss the simple dishes very much: the herring, the boiled eggs, the potatoes, the onion, the radish. And although they are simple to prepare I can never quite replicate them. Sometimes Grandma would prepare *kholodich,* calf's foot jelly, and on rare occasions even a glass of "drink" would be added, or schnapps—which is what Grandpa Aharon called the cheap brandy reserved for special occasions.

But this time there was a surprise. When the meal was set before us, Abigail removed a small flask from her pack, placed it on the table, and said a Russian word that needs no translation to any language: "Vodka."

Grandma Tonia was so thrilled that she whispered to me, "This one, don't change like socks. You can bring her here one more time." Then she said, "Just a moment," and she stood up and left the room.

I was surprised. I had never before seen her show any interest in drinking.

"Where did she go?" Abigail whispered.

"I have no idea," I whispered back.

From deep inside the house came the sound of a key turning in a lock and a door opening and suddenly the air was sodden with an old, strange smell, both pleasant and unpleasant, a smell I recalled from those days when she would ask me to remove chairs from the forbidden rooms without scritching the walls. I knew she had opened the Holy of Holies, and I wondered whether she liked Abigail so much that she had decided to let us sleep on the big old double bed, the one with the tall metal headboard painted dark brown.

We did not merit the bed, but Grandma Tonia returned to the kitchen carrying three shot glasses and said that if there was vodka then one should drink it in proper fashion.

We drank, I in three small, cautious sips, the women—the young one, the old one—in one swift gulp with a sharp snap of the head. I had never before seen my grandmother drinking like that and understood that her world was bigger and deeper than I had imagined and I was only familiar with the little bit that stuck out. She slammed her empty glass to the table in a manner that sounded like an extension of her Russian accent, stared at Abigail, and said to me, "Ask her what she does."

"I don't need to ask. I know what she does," I said. "She studies education in America."

"And how old is she?"

"Three years older than I."

Grandma Tonia grew worried. "Does she have children?" she asked, eager to know already, at this early stage, before fate struck our family in my generation as well.

"No."

"Did you ask her?"

"I'm telling you, she doesn't. And anyway, what does it matter? She has a boyfriend she's planning to marry next summer."

"Tell her to stay here with you. She is nice. She's a *mutzlach*."

"What are you two talking about?" Abigail asked.

"Ask her what her father does," my grandmother said, changing the subject.

"Abigail," I said, "my grandmother would like to know what your father does."

"My father," said Abigail, shifting her gaze from me to my grandmother, "has a General Electric dealership in Los Angeles. In fact," she added, "his is one of the biggest GE dealerships on the entire West Coast."

28

"That's what she said to you?" my mother asked. " 'My father has one of the biggest General Electric dealerships in Los Angeles'? She said it to you but she was looking at my mother?"

This was a special moment, a wonderful first. Me telling my mother a story about her mother, and not her telling me.

"This is how it was," I responded with pride, even mimicking the accent.

"And my mother? What did she say?"

"Nothing. But I thought I saw something light up in her eyes. Or maybe it only seems that way now because of what happened after that."

Did I really see something? Was there a flicker in my grandmother's eyes? I don't know, but even if there was, it was extinguished and disappeared at once. I told her it was late and we were tired from the trip and wanted to shower before bed. To my surprise she said we could use the indoor shower.

"Are you sure?" I asked.

"It's in her honor, not yours."

"I'd actually rather shower in the cowshed," I said. "In your 'excellent shower.' "

"What are you two talking about?" Abigail asked.

"About what I explained before, that at my grandmother's you shower in the cowshed," I told her.

"What are you two talking about?" my grandmother asked.

"She said it's fine. She doesn't want to dirty your shower," I told her.

Grandma Tonia smiled and nearly winked at me. She stood up and brought us two rough, old towels and a kerosene lantern because "there's no reason to light up all the electricity in the cowshed and wake up all the cows."

"I told you this is how it would be," I whispered to Abigail, "and you didn't believe me. You thought I was just making up stories. But now you're going to shower with the cows."

It was a hot, clear night. A full moon had already completed a third of its climb over the dome of the heavens. The cows breathed moistly in their pen. I hung the lantern on a nail and told Abigail the story known to everyone in Nahalal, about the old man who hung his burning kerosene lantern on a fly standing on the wall and burned down his barn.

She laughed loudly, took off her clothes, and hung them on another nail. Then she spun slowly in place by the cowshed wall while I, hose in hand, showered her.

"Strip down and join me already," she said. "There's lots of space under the hose and enough flies on the wall for your clothes, too."

When we came back to the house wrapped in towels, Grandma Tonia had already prepared our *mishkav* for us, and all at once that nice expression shed its innocent memories of childhood and the lovely Ibn Ezra poem and overflowed with excitement and passion. She led us to the room, opened the door, told us to have a good time, and left.

Abigail, whose jollity just kept growing, asked if she had bid us good night.

I told her one could understand it that way, too, but that my grandmother had actually said, "Have a good time."

She said, "I don't believe it."

"That's what she said, and she meant every word of it."

The room had not changed from the time I slept there the previous time or the very first time. There was the same bookshelf holding the same volumes of *The Young Laborer* and old copies of the children's supplement of the *Davar* newspaper, the same pleasant old sheets, and folding wooden shutters, and screen windows that needed tightening, the same freckled floor tiles, shiny from so many washings and polishings, the same rustling of cypress branches from the trees my grandfather planted, which still stood along the pathway leading to the yard. From one of them came that same eerie rasping, though the barn owl was a different barn owl, not the same one that had frightened me as a boy of five when I slept in that very same room. Perhaps that barn owl's great-grandchild.

The old metal cot creaked. Abigail and I laughed noiselessly. I am not inclined to share the details of such events, not in my fictional work and not in this true story. But I will mention that Abigail was only with me then for several days, after which she returned to her life. We were nothing more than an amorous, passing adventure for each other, but on that night, whose unbelievable climax is yet to come, I loved her truly, and her embraces said the same.

We loved and we laughed and we looked at each other up close and we had fun with "now I see you and you don't see me, now you see me and I don't see you" and other secret amusements of the nearsighted. And after I translated for her the Nahum Gutman comics that appeared at the end of the old *Davar* supplement for children, we fell asleep as we were, naked, our limbs splayed, uncovered. And that is how my grandmother found us when, at three o'clock in the morning she opened the door and entered the room.

She did not knock and I did not sense her presence, but Abigail sprang awake and raised the sheet from the floor and wrapped herself in it before she sat up and elbowed me in the ribs. It took a few seconds for me to gather my wits and comprehend that the blurry figure in a white nightgown was not someone in my dream but Grandma Tonia herself, in person, and that I was naked as the day I was born while she was wearing a nightgown she had probably sewn from one of the old sheets that would also never be thrown away. But once I had sat up in bed and put on my glasses in order to understand what was happening, I was no longer interested in her or her clothing, because in the shadow behind her, I had only just noticed, stood a large and shiny creature in the darkness.

29

My heart stopped for a moment. All at once I understood that I was looking at the legendary vacuum cleaner, Grandma Tonia's sweeper, which had emerged from our Narnia behind the bathroom door, from the land of family fables. It had come out of its box, peeled off its shrouds, and become real before my very eyes. Here it was: the proof, the thing itself. Not a dream and not an optical illusion. Not the little sweeper from Uncle Yeshayahu's visit in the 1950s but the big sweeper of that small globe and the yellow pencil and the capacious ocean, New York, Tel El Shamam, white, green, earth, spotted, blue, red polka dots. This is how it was, in all its fine details. My mother was right.

Grandma Tonia stepped into the middle of the room, the vacuum cleaner following behind. Neither one made a noise. She was small and barefoot, while it was as big as a cow but quiet as a cat on its black rubber wheels. The nightgown shone white. The chrome sparkled. The canister was indeed as big as a barrel. The black suction tube, at least as thick as my arm, hung limply from her hand, only hinting at its power.

Although I was completely naked I will freeze this frame for a moment because, before I continue, there is one more thing I must explain: more than once a suspicion had stolen its way into my heart that what was at stake was not merely different versions of a single story but one true story from which myths sprouted the way offshoots do around pomegranate and olive trees. If that was the case, I reasoned, then, as was true with other mythologies, some of our family stories—or perhaps most of them—were not "this is how it was." Grandpa Aharon had only intended to kill himself in the Kishon River, not the Jordan. Gypsies had not kidnapped Uncle Yitzhak, he had run away with them. Ah, our jennet, was indeed intelligent, but not as smart as the stories would have us believe, so she had never used a little piece of metal wire to pick a lock, she had merely stolen the key from Grandfather's pocket. Maybe she had not even flown in the air, and if she had, she'd gotten only as far as Kfar Yehoshua. And since I had my doubts about all these tales, I had shrunk the image of the vacuum cleaner in my consciousness. But now it suddenly became clear that my mother had also done the same thing, because the real live vacuum cleaner was several times larger and more impressive than its story version.

One way or the other, in the presence of the vacuum cleaner—whose curvaceous canister and comely tube had taken shape before my very eyes—and Abigail's body heat, which informed me that I was fully conscious, I felt a true feeling of uplift. This was how Heinrich Schliemann felt when he proved the veracity of Homer's writings by exposing and identifying the ruins of Troy. This is how the archaeologists who one day will find the Ark of the Covenant and Noah's Ark will feel.

But Grandma Tonia was not thinking about all the historicophilosophical and cognitive meanings of the emergence of her sweeper. "Ask her," she said to me, ignoring the situation, the nakedness, the bed, as if we were still sitting in her kitchen eating herring and drinking vodka and chatting, "ask her if her father can get me a little sealing ring for this svieeperrr."

I could not believe my ears. "Grandma," I said, astonished, "that's why you barged in here in the middle of the night without knocking? For some part you need for your old sweeper? Do you know what time it is?"

185

"It's a very small part and I didn't barge in in the middle," she said. "I heard when it was all over and I gave you enough time to rest and calm down."

Abigail was stunned. She whispered, "What's happening? Is that the vacuum cleaner she doesn't use? What does she want?"

"She wants your father to get her some part for this vacuum cleaner," I told her. "Tell her there's no chance, otherwise we'll never get back to sleep. And give me a corner of the sheet. I can't lie here like this in front of her."

"Tell her it's something small," my grandmother said. "A broken sealing ring that doesn't seal properly. I need a replacement."

"How do you know that?" I asked. "You only used the sweeper for one week."

"Two," she said. "Two weeks. And I know it because that's what Yitzhak told me, and Yitzhak is an almost engineer and he understands such things. He took the svieeperrr apart and he checked it and he said that one day, a lot of years later, this sealing ring would not work properly and dirt would escape."

"But why is it so important to you right now?"

"It's important because Yitzhak said it would happen a lot of years later, and already nearly forty years have passed."

This smelted logic of hers convinced me. "She needs to replace a sealing ring on this vacuum cleaner," I told Abigail, "and she's asking that your father get it for her."

Abigail rose from the bed, pulled the sheet to her body, and secured it. She approached the sweeper, bent down, and examined it. I remained in bed, my heart full of joy. Few pairs of lovers are lucky enough to enjoy such a rousing and special first night together: the wee hours of the night, a full moon waning outside and shining through the slats of the shutters, the male lover sprawled naked on the bed, his grandmother standing nearby while his beloved, with only a sheet pulled to her

186

body, leans over and inspects an ancient vacuum cleaner whose existence has only just this minute been proven and yet which already needs a new sealing ring! What could be better?

"Do me a favor," I said to Abigail. "Tell her it's an old appliance, that there's no getting the spare parts anywhere. That way she'll leave the room and you'll come back to bed."

Grandma Tonia got angry. She did not understand the words I had spoken to Abigail but their tone was absolutely clear to her.

"What are you saying to her?" she demanded, but Abigail had already lost interest in me and was concentrating solely on Grandma Tonia and her sweeper.

"Tell her," she said, straightening herself to her full height and speaking to me but looking at Grandma Tonia, "that my father would be very happy to display this appliance in the window of his dealership in Los Angeles. There is no such vacuum cleaner in the entire United States that is so old and in mint condition. Tell her that if she gives it to me my father will send her a new and modern sweeper in its place."

"Abigail," I said, "it's not 'sweeper,' it's 'svieeperrr.' You've got to improve your accent."

"What are you people talking about there?" my grandmother asked again in her usual mixture of suspicion and anger upon hearing my imitation of her.

I related Abigail's offer to her, and she only grew more suspicious. Her sweeper would travel to America? He would send her a new one? When? How exactly? And anyway, she would not be willing to part with this one until the new one had arrived.

"Grandma," I told her, "you're living in the Dark Ages. Packages come on airplanes, and there are couriers that deliver to your house. The package from Abigail's father will come straight from his office in America to your doorstep. All you have to do is shout to the deliveryman, 'Around back! Come in the second door!' And anyway, why do you always think people are trying to rip you off?"

"Tell her," said Abigail, who wished to retain the momentum that had been created, as far as she was concerned, for negotiations, "that my father will throw in another General Electric appliance with the new sweeper. A small gift: a blender, a toaster oven, a hair dryer. Whatever she wants."

That voice, which only an hour earlier had whispered sweet nothings into my neck, had become decisive, even a little curt. I translated her offer, and my grandmother grew even more suspicious. "What's a *toaster oven*? I don't need something that my grandson doesn't even know how to translate."

At that, she turned around and began to leave the room, her sweeper close behind: obedient, servile, but still full of hope.

"Detain her," Abigail said.

"Grandma," I called out, "wait a second."

She stopped.

"Abigail wants to tell you something else."

"Tell her," said Abigail, "that my father will also be happy to pay her. In addition to the new vacuum cleaner that she will receive and the little gift, he'll give her five hundred dollars for her old appliance. I am willing to write the check right now."

This time it was in my own heart that a suspicion arose. This nice, peach-smelling, amusing girl, full of humor and passion, whom I had met at the post office in Mahane Yehuda in Jerusalem and whose spine started so attractively at the nape of her neck and extended so beautifully to her tailbone, had suddenly become a haggling, greedy-eyed speculator.

I grew a little resentful, too. "You've got a checkbook with that kind of money and we're traveling on buses and showering with cows?" I said, reproachful.

"Seven hundred and fifty," she said.

"Grandma," I said, "in addition to all kinds of gifts and a

brand-new vacuum cleaner, Abigail is offering you seven hundred and fifty dollars for your old and broken-down sweeper, and I think I can get you an even better deal. So if you take her up on it I think I deserve a small cut."

"Your translation was a lot longer than my offer," Abigail said. "What exactly did you add?"

"We were talking about the cash incentive you offered."

"Tell her a thousand, and that includes a ten percent cut for you."

"It's already up to a thousand," I told Grandma Tonia. "And in addition to my cut I demand permission to take a bath in your locked bathroom."

"Under no circumstances," she said. Then she asked, "Is that new dollars or old dollars?"

"What's she saying?" Abigail asked. "What kind of dollars is she talking about?"

"I don't think she really understands the difference between rubles and dollars," I told her. I explained to my grandmother that the dollar was not affected by the murder of Czar Nikolai II by the Bolsheviks, and then I restated the offer.

"How much is that in liras?" she asked.

I converted it for her. I no longer remember what the sum was, but it was very large, both to an old farm wife like herself and to a young ambulance driver like myself, who was also forced to raise white mice for a living. But the moment I told her what the sum was, my grandmother said, "If she's willing to pay that much money for my old svieeperrr then it's clearly worth a lot more than she's offering."

Just then Abigail, who did not understand what we were talking about and did not know my grandmother all that well, made a big mistake. "Tell her," she said, "that I want her to operate it for me right now, because I want to make sure it works."

"You're making a mistake," I told her.

"Business is business," she responded. "I insist."

"Grandma," I said, "she asks you to turn it on because she wants to make sure it works. So I'm confirming the deal: a thousand dollars. You and I will discuss the matter of my bath, just the two of us, when she's gone."

"No chance," my grandmother said. "The bath will get dirty and I'll have to clean it. And the svieeperrr will get dirty and I don't know how to take it apart, and then I won't be able to fall asleep until Yitzhak comes. I'm an old woman and Yitzhak isn't so young anymore either and even this svieeperrr is no baby."

I began to laugh. The two women gazed at me with four astonished eyes. This was business, a serious matter. What was there to laugh about؟

"Tell her I want to see it and hear it working," Abigail repeated. "And I want to see it vacuum."

I repeated this to my grandmother and added, "You don't even need Uncle Yitzhak. Show Abigail that the sweeper works and she'll take it with her, dirt and all. A thousand dollars for this old piece of junk is a lot of money. Just dump a little dirt on the floor and show her that it works."

Words are capable of stronger action than the reality they are describing, and in this case it became apparent that the mistake I had made was even greater than Abigail's. The words "dump" and "dirt" and "floor" had such a strong effect on Grandma Tonia that she could not listen to the voice of reason. Dump dirt on her floor؟ Hers؟ Dirt on her floor؟ No, no, and no! Not for all the money in the world! She had already turned on her heels and was on her way out of the room, the sweeper dragging along behind her, looking back in despair and clueless about what had happened.

"What happened؟" Abigail whispered. "Tell her to come back!"

"It was my turn to make a mistake," I told her. "We both screwed up, each one of us in turn. You have no idea how badly."

"Stop, please, stop!" Abigail called out.

Grandma Tonia turned and glared at her. She said exactly what I knew she would, then left the room. I shrank in the bed.

"What did she say?" Abigail said, taken aback.

I knew it was all over, there was no chance. I heard the key open the bathroom door. Several minutes passed during which I knew that my grandmother was returning the poor vacuum cleaner to its box-prison, then covering it with the same old prison uniform it had been bound up in for forty years.

"What did she say?" Abigail asked once again.

"She said, '*At ponit elai?*' " I told her.

"What's that? Talk English, please."

"It's something like 'You talkin' to me?' " I said.

Abigail tackled me on the bed, pinning me down. She hissed, " 'You talkin' to me?' That's what she said? You ruined everything! I wanted to bring my father a present."

Outside, I could hear the key turning in the lock of the bathroom door. I squeezed Abigail in a big hug. Soon, my grandmother would set out on her workday and she would pull the mattress out from under us: Up, up, stop stinking up the bed. I need to start cleaning. There's a lot of work to be done.

The first rays of sun pierced the shutters. "Look," I said to Abigail, and showed her the dance of the dust in its light. We got up and enjoyed a morning hike through the fields, then came back to the house to take our leave of Grandma Tonia and thank her. Abigail told her in flowing English that if she ever changed her mind she should let me know and I would inform her; Grandma smiled warmly and did not even ask me to translate. We went to eat breakfast at the home of Yair and Tzilla, and from there we went down to the main road to catch a bus for the next part of our trip.

We spent several happy and pleasant days together, after which I escorted Abigail to the airport. She flew home, to her father and her boyfriend, while I went back to my ambulance and my mice and my studies. We never saw each other again.

Occasionally I wonder: Where is she today? What became of her? Did she marry that boyfriend, the one to whom she sent a package that caused us to meet? Does she work at what she studied, special education? Or maybe she is living with a female partner in Berkeley? Perhaps she has a turkey farm in Illinois, and seven children fathered by her first three husbands? One thing is clear to me: she went back to America without my grandmother's sweeper, but with one of her very best expressions.

30

Some two years later I completed my studies at university. For a little while longer I worked at the Magen David Adom station and then at Israel Television, where I was employed as a research assistant for documentary programming.

Several years after that I began appearing on television as well. At the time, there was only one television station in Israel, which meant that every bit of nonsense broadcast enjoyed a 100 percent viewer rating. It did not take Grandma Tonia long to discover that her eldest grandson's face was well known, and she was not hesitant at all about letting everyone hear about it. When she traveled by bus, she announced it to the driver. When she went to some government office, she made it known to the clerk there. When she went for a medical checkup, she informed the doctor, the nurse, the X-ray technician, the laboratory assistant, and the other patients in the waiting room. When I commented on this she got angry at me: it was her right; I was her grandson.

I was not the only family member to make her angry. At the same time, the matter of the "album" arose, over which she lost a lot of sleep. This memorial book was the album of the Second Aliyah, which was being edited just then. The editors wished to gather in a single volume the photographs of all the pioneers of the Second Aliyah, under which they would add several biographical details. Grandma Tonia understood at once that her late sister, Shoshanna, and not she herself, would be commemorated in the album next to Grandpa Aharon, and this drove her into a rage.

For good reason I have used the word "commemorated," because it is precisely the word that she used. "I want commemoration" she kept declaring, though to others this meant commemoration among the pioneers of the nation and founders of the State of Israel, while for Grandma Tonia this meant something far more important: the recognition of her status at Grandpa Aharon's side and in the annals of our family history.

She went immediately to her brother Moshe and demanded that he make use of all his good connections and friends so that she would appear next to her husband in the album. As noted earlier, Uncle Moshe would write letters to the head of the Labor Movement pointing out the cracks that formed in the fortified ideological wall of our path; in her opinion, a single letter to David Ben-Gurion would cause the prime minister to intervene with his characteristic assertiveness and decisiveness. Just as he had given the order to fire on the *Altalena,* a ship bringing Etzel fighters, weapons, and hundreds of new immigrants to Israel shortly after the establishment of the state, so too would he give the order to include her in the album.

Uncle Moshe laughed and said, "First of all, Tonichka, men

of Ben-Gurion's caliber do not occupy themselves with such trivial matters. And second, there is one other small problem: you cannot possibly appear in the album of the Second Aliyah for the same reason that Yitzhak and I cannot, namely because we all came here during the third wave of immigration. There is no reason to be angry with me; we were not in the album of the First Aliyah either and we won't be in the album of the French National Assembly for the very same reason."

Such weak excuses had never interested Grandma Tonia, and the word "trivial" offended her; nor did her brother's calling her by the diminutive Tonichka please her. Anyone unwilling to come swiftly to his sister's aid had no right to call her by her nickname.

She was already considering granting him the title "my brother no longer," but she decided instead to give him one more chance: "You just write to Ben-Gurion about this album and he will decide if this is a trivial matter or not."

To Uncle Moshe's great fortune—if not to the former prime minister's—Ben-Gurion died a few days after that conversation. Sometime later a compromise was settled upon: Shoshanna's photograph would appear in the album, but not next to Grandpa Aharon. He was already too old and tired to express his opinion, and in the end seven pages came between Aharon and Shoshanna, a reasonable distance between a man married for a second time and his first wife. Grandma Tonia was forced to accept this decision but was not fully satisfied. A number of times she reiterated that she was in need of true "commemoration"—which is to say, she and Grandpa Aharon—and in the end, it was I who took care of it.

The opportunity arose when Israel Television was working on a historical series about the rise of Zionism, called *Pillar of Fire,* at a time when the research assistants were occupied with the second and third waves of immigration and the settling of the Jezreel Valley. The producer, Naomi Kaplansky, who was in charge of organizing and editing interviews for the series, asked if I knew any Nahalal old-timers who might be good at telling about those times.

Without batting an eye or hesitating, I said, "My grandmother!"

"Your grandmother? Who is she? What did she do?"

"She worked. She milked, cleaned, cooked. She told me stories, and she managed the farm and the family."

"And she'll be able to tell about the history of the settling of the Jezreel Valley, and about ideology in that period?"

"As for the history," I said, "there are enough versions already, so there will be one more—hers. As for the ideology, she'll show you new sides to ideology that you never even dreamed existed."

Naomi Kaplansky said that with all due respect to my nonobjective recommendations, she had never heard of my grandmother.

"Grandma Tonia," I told her. "Tonia Ben-Barak. Now you've heard of her."

She laughed, then told me that the following week she would be traveling to the Jezreel Valley to meet Meir Yaari and Yaacov Hazan, the leaders of the Mapam, and if she had time she would pay a visit to my grandmother as well and check her out.

Quickly, I let my grandmother know that her commemoration was on its way, that a Ms. Kaplansky from Israel Television would be stopping by, and that she should act according to the following instructions:

Do not tell anyone in the village about the upcoming visit by Ms. Kaplansky.

Do not complain to Ms. Kaplansky about the album of the Second Aliyah.

Tell Ms. Kaplansky stories that begin with the words, "When I was a young girl . . ."

Do not complain to Ms. Kaplansky about Grandpa Aharon's "runoffs" or that Menahem and Yair did not separate the cream for you or that they did not tell you they were going to Haifa.

Do not seat Ms. Kaplansky on the bench on the porch; hold the meeting inside the house.

Furthermore, Grandma, and this is important: Ms. Kaplansky will be making a long journey. If necessary, please let her use the toilet. Whatever you do, do not send her out to water the special citrus tree planted by Grandpa.

Like Abigail, Naomi Kaplansky returned from her meeting completely enchanted by Grandma Tonia. "She's a real character, your grandmother," Naomi said. "A little meshugeneh, but not completely crazy, either—an original, with an interesting take on things. And what herring she makes . . ."

And so it was that in that outstanding series *Pillar of Fire,* in the stirring episode called "The Valley Is a Dream," Grandma Tonia was the only interviewee from Nahalal. Not the usual suspects, the ones who always represented the village: not the people of vision, morals, and action; not the activists, the politicos, the *machers;* not the ideologues, the self-confident, the makers of the constitution, the actualizers. Instead, just Grandma Tonia, the Grandma Tonia whose genetic material was passed down to me, causing me to appear with red nail polish on my toenails in front of those very same people, at the inauguration of the old arms cache used by the Haganah.

Naomi Kaplansky had asked her, among other things, about the differences between the moshav and the kibbutz. Instead of lecturing about the "collective" versus the "individual," about socialism and the religion of labor, she analyzed the entire issue from a very natural and logical point of view, that of the family. "We went to a moshav because we wanted freedom and privacy," she explained, that incorrigible individualist, adding a sharp statistical observation: "A lot of people left the kibbutzim and went to moshavim. Nobody left the moshav for a kibbutz."

As for the historical ideological conflict between the two types of settlement, a conflict that many had flogged before her, she said something quite simple: On a moshav you know who you are sitting down to eat with—your family, for better or worse. But in a kibbutz collective dining hall sometimes you may find yourself with people you do not wish to sit next to, in whose company you do not wish to eat.

But all this was not important. What was truly important was that in *Pillar of Fire*　both the televised version and the book that followed—there appeared a wonderful photograph of Grandma Tonia and Grandpa Aharon, a good-looking young couple emanating passion and love. She is sitting on the ground, her hair in braids, smiling, while he, far taller and more handsome than she, is leaning over her from behind, holding her wrist, nearly pressed up against her back, and both look as though they are waiting for the photographer to finish his work so that they can go back to their lovemaking on the threshing floor or the vineyard or the bed.

The people of the Jezreel Valley were up in arms, the village in turmoil. Tonia Ben-Barak of all people should represent the first workers' moshav on the flagship television program about Zionism? Grandma Tonia was angry, too, but as always, according to her own logic: "She didn't film the porch for me," she complained to me about Naomi Kaplansky after the broadcast, "and I washed it especially for her."

But she was grateful to me, and I was reinstated as her favored grandchild. "Now she'll let you take a bath in her locked

Tonia and Aharon

bathroom, too," my aunt Batsheva, the proud mother of Nadav, said with a laugh. But I was already beyond such trivialities, or at least I pretended to be.

31

Grandpa Aharon died in 1978. Many and bad were the days of his life. He was eighty-nine years old at the time of his death, and he had not known enough happiness or experienced enough pleasure when he passed away owing all his grandchildren gifts for finding the *afikomen* that he hid each year at Passover. I asked to receive what I was owed from his inheritors, Menahem and Yair, but they said they were still waiting for the *afikomen* gifts he owed them. So I asked Grandma Tonia, and she repeated her old motto: "You're not going to inherit me as long as I'm alive!"

Incidentally, the *afikomen* that he hid in Aunt Batsheva's house that no one managed to find was finally discovered several years after his death, when Batsheva decided to move a picture on the wall and the missing piece of matza fell to the floor—the *afikomen* of 1963 had been found! And as happens in our family, the matter gave rise to an abundance of stories and tears and jokes, but there was no longer anyone from whom a prize could be demanded.

Grandma Tonia died nine years after Grandpa, at the age of eighty-four. Her final days were difficult ones. But so were the ones that came beforehand, so why should the last ones be different? She complained and accused even more than usual, bringing up memories that only she remembered and picking at scabs that were better left to heal and disappear.

Her health deteriorated rapidly. Years of hard labor, stress, and anger took their toll. She spent only a short amount of time in a nursing home not far from Nahalal, and I visited her there on several occasions. She asked me to take her home, to her house. She pleaded and sobbed but I could not do what she wanted. She died several weeks later, and the entire family gathered for her funeral.

The funerals in our family—with the exception of the horrible military burials—are always characterized by some strange or amusing occurrence that causes people to smile and even laugh in the midst of their tears. For example, at the funeral for Uncle Menahem, who was a man with a sense of humor, we all cried, but we told his jokes and performed his imitations and laughed the way we did in his company. At Grandpa Aharon's funeral, the wife of his friend Nahum Sneh, a member of the Makarovite Trio, gave a splendid performance of curses, accusations, and reprimands meant for the entire family unto the tenth generation, until Grandma Tonia shut her up by saying, "But why are you doing this in front of everyone? Come visit me afterward, we'll drink tea and talk." And everyone chuckled.

At my mother's funeral everyone was stricken and stunned. She was sixty-four at her death, the first of the seven siblings. In many ways my mother was the pillar around which they revolved, and her death smashed their very foundations. The funeral was large and very bitter. All the family members, her friends from Jerusalem and the Jezreel Valley, her students past and present, came to her funeral at the Nahalal cemetery and walked about stooped and silent, then gathered around the grave dug for her, and no one had the strength to speak because it was too painful.

It seemed that no one would be smiling at this funeral, but then suddenly a mysterious older man jumped out from the crowd, someone whom most of those present did not know, and waved his hand dramatically and shouted, "Batya!"

Everyone fell silent. The man paused momentarily, displaying experience with eulogies and acting, and shouted again: "I am Uncle Yasha!"

We breathed a sigh of relief—there would be a show after all! We allowed Uncle Yasha to deliver his eulogy, which he did exceptionally well and with quite a bit of pathos. The crowd whispered, offered suggestions about who this Yasha was: Had Grandpa Aharon hidden another brother from us? Some claimed they actually knew him and that his name really was Yasha, and in the end we decided that the title "uncle" suited him, even though the Batya he had in mind was a different Batya.

My sister, brother, and I did not make him stop. We felt

he was having a good effect on us and on the other mourners. He spoke floridly and with emotion that did the trick. After he had uttered no more than a few sentences, glances and winks were exchanged as well as a few more hypotheses about Yasha, and here and there someone laughed audibly so that even my mother got her funeral with smiles, as is proper.

And at every one of our funerals we repeat what Grandma Tonia used to say: "She is no longer," to which she would add, "and it was a terrible death." Which is precisely what we said about her at her funeral. We mentioned other phrases she had coined and some people even imitated her, out of habit. Near the hole dug next to Grandpa Aharon's grave that awaited her body—as short and small as she was in life, she was even tinier now in death—stood her sons, Micha, Menahem, and Yair, with their wives and children. Her siblings came as well; Moshe had predeceased her but Yitzhak and Yaacov were there, sad and old and too weak to stand. Yaacov cried bitterly. Yitzhak was silent, but his blue eyes were red.

A little farther off, near the fence, stood Grandpa Aharon's sons Binya and Itamar and their families; Batya and Batsheva stood right at the edge of the grave. They had long since left home and the village, trailing long and painful umbilical cords and stories after them, but now they were once again her two little girls.

They cried. Batsheva said, "Now you'll always be with Father," and my mother read something she had prepared in advance. I include it here as written, without any changes or editing. This is exactly, precisely the eulogy she gave, and since it was written down and preserved, no one can confront it with some other version:

Our mother did not come to Israel in the Second Aliyah, nor was she among the founders of Nahalal. She arrived after the Russian Revolution, with her mother, her younger brother, and a cousin to reunite with the rest of the family here in the Land of Israel. All she knew about Nahalal was from rumors; she had two older brothers here and a brother-in-law, Aharon Ben-Barak, whom she had last seen when she was a girl of six or seven and he brought her a doll when he came to visit the family in their Russian village.

When she arrived in Nahalal there were already huts and cowsheds, and people received a little sugar and oil on credit from what was known as "the warehouse." In summer there was nowhere to hide from the blazing sun and in winter there was mud up to the knees. She was a young girl, as she liked to say: "When I was a young girl . . . " still wearing her brown school pinafore and a black bow in her hair, when she came to this new world, this different, unfamiliar world, difficult and even cruel.

She did not work at Hulda or Be'er Yaacov, she did not help establish Deganya or plow the fields at Sejera or Yavniel. She simply came to her family at Nahalal and began a new life, grappling on a daily basis with family difficulties she did not know how to cope with, and social criticism, for her desire to beautify, decorate, and just be different.

She was difficult and demanding of herself, difficult and demanding of others. She was jealous, unforgiving, and tenacious, but she kept on working, taking upon herself the burdens from sunrise to nighttime: the grape harvest and fruit picking, the season of pickling olives and cucumbers, the manufacture of jams under the pomegranate tree in the yard, and when money was scarce, she took on work outside the house: she housed and fed the electric company workers when they came to put electricity in Nahalal, and in an old notepad I found an "accounting for forest workers," a penny and a half, and another half penny, and twenty mil, the price of meals they ate at her table. The farm became a part of her, her personality and her property, the corner of the world where she could do what she wanted. From the time I was a child I knew: if it weren't for Mother, it was not at all certain we would have stayed on in Nahalal.

There was a lovely, gracious side to her as well. How we all loved her stories about her family and friends back in Russia, about her grandfather with the estate who was hanged by rioting mobs, about her mother, a woman of valor who received sacks of flour straight from the trains at the entrance to her shop. We sang songs in Russian even before we joined the youth movement. We were enchanted by her rich language, the beautiful expressions she used, her stories, her longing.

There, on the cement platform outside the kitchen, that hot cement platform we would wash and clean and wash and clean, she would sit with us and tell us stories and sing and bring all of us into her secret world of wonders, that only a few knew existed.

Mother, Father, you lie there now together in everlasting serenity. No more anger, no more outbursts, at peace with one another and in the true love that was shaken to its core and shattered in the land of the living, and which now comes to its true and final resting place.

When old people are buried, especially those who were particularly difficult during their lifetimes or caused their relatives to wait too long before they finally died, there is sometimes a feeling of relief. But that is not the way we felt at Grandma Tonia's funeral. Everyone knew she was not an easy woman, that she was stubborn, vindictive, jealous, obsessive, and excessively demanding. But in some ways she was the purified essence of us all, for better and worse, the essence that was never diluted in the water of surrender or compromise.

She was our source of strength, the one who fought and struggled, the one who did not "runoff" and did not leave, and she held on to the farm by her fingernails, truly with her ten fingers. "*Ah-nu,* go ahead, touch them," she said at one of our final meetings as she spread her fingers out before me—or, more precisely, tried to spread them. They were so gnarled, heart-wrenchingly so, especially the pinky finger, which could no longer stretch out along a glass of tea. "*Ah-nu,* touch them, touch them, see how tired they are, and full of pain."

When the funeral ended we all came down from the cemetery to the village and sat on the porch outside the house. Even then, when she was dead, no one dared enter the house itself, not from the front door and not from the second door, lest she come and take chunks out of us. Like the Children of Israel before entering the Red Sea, each of us waited for a Nachshon to go first and open the door.

We were very, very sad. We did not feel the relief we had expected, or the pain of regret, or the shame of acceptance. So, we did what our family always does, in good times and bad—we told stories. We told stories about her and about Grandpa, about the village and the family, and we argued whether this is how it was or this is how it wasn't, knowing all the while that even that moment would become a story with at least six different versions.

All at once, my mother and Aunt Batsheva, Tonia's two daughters, got to their feet and opened the door and entered the house. Everyone fell silent, exchanging glances, and then we stood up as one and followed them inside until the house was full of people. We suddenly realized how small and meager it was. For many years we had not entered it; being forbidden

204

made it more beautiful, as prohibitions often do. Longing, as longing does, made it more elegant. Memory, as memories do, made it far larger than it was. My mother and my aunt passed through the dining room where no one ate and reached the door that no one entered, then turned left and stood in front of the locked rooms, Grandma Tonia's temple.

The door was closed, of course. Questions arose: Where is the key? A ruckus ensued, with everyone searching in drawers and kitchen cupboards, but no key turned up. My mother and her sister went out to the toolshed, where long ago they had been raised with their brothers all crammed into a single room, and then later it became the hangout, where a wild, happy gang that included Uncle Micha and his friends spent time, and still later Uncle Menahem's room, and finally a rickety shed that held tools and all manner of things that moshavniks cannot part with because they never throw anything away since if you throw it away then tomorrow you will realize it was exactly what you needed.

But the key was not there, either. A few people claimed that Grandma Tonia had managed to sneak it into the grave with her. Others thought we should break down the door. But my mother returned to the door, removed the rag from the handle, and pressed it. To everyone's surprise the door was closed but not locked. It opened wide.

Noses sniffed. Eyes penetrated. Ears tilted inward. Details from the stories we had heard were proven true: the cool silence, the watery air, the transparent gloom, the absolute cleanliness. This is how it was. Here were the tattered sheets on her furniture.

Batsheva and Batya entered her forbidden rooms and opened the windows she had shut. Light and air poured in, and with them more faces of more family members, some crowding into the doorway, others stepping outside to look in from the sidewalk through the windows that had been opened. And at once, along with the inquisitive eyes, there was an invasion by grains of dust and needles from the casuarina trees and bird feathers and pollen and flying seeds and dust motes that had been waiting for years on the other side of the wall for just this moment, and they dirtied her spotless temple.

And then something unbelievable happened, but this is how it was: my mother and my aunt tore away the old sheets that covered the sofa and the armchairs and the crafted cupboards, and as if they had planned it years in advance and had given long thought and consideration to the matter and perhaps had even staged a few real or imaginary rehearsals and had discussed it during the funeral, the two of them raised the hems of their skirts, climbed onto Grandma Tonia's sofa, and began to jump up and down.

Even those of us who were there found it hard to believe that that was what was happening, not to mention those who were not. But that is how it was. They jumped on her sofa and they jumped on her armchairs and they jumped on her buffet table and back to the sofa, and they did not stop jumping on her furniture, screaming and laughing, until they fell on the large double bed with the tall metal headboard painted dark brown to resemble wood, and hugged each other and cried.

32

While everyone else was watching my mother and her sister jumping on their mother's furniture and sprawling on her bed and dirtying it with their tears, I slipped away to the Holy of Holies, the bathroom.

Here, too, the door was closed but not locked. I turned on the light and was nearly blinded by the pure whiteness of the walls, the shine of the bathtub, the sparkle of all the ceramic. According to all accounts, Nadav was the last person to visit here, and Grandma would have cleaned the place thoroughly after his soak in the tub. There was not even a single stain, no mark, no grain of dust in the room. But there was also no vacuum cleaner; her sweeper was gone. Just then, however, I spotted the German beer stein she had refused to give me during her lifetime, standing in the middle of the bathroom and waiting for me with a tearful smile. "You can inherit me now. She is no longer."

Just as I bent down to pick it up I sensed a hush had fallen on the house, a silence so deep that I could hear it in my entire body, not just my ears. I turned around, the beer stein in my hand, and here they all were, the family, standing in silence, awaiting an answer.

"It's not here," I said, crestfallen.

In our family, stories are told and then they disseminate themselves, some by air, some by clinging to clothing, and still others by our own special digestive system: they are swallowed into the pores and secreted by way of our mouths. There are not many secrets, quite certainly not when the bathroom door is wide open. The story of Abigail, in all its details, including the sums of money discussed—especially those—was known to one and all. And not only known, it had already elicited ornamentation, new versions, and additions.

Everyone glared accusingly at me. Some of my family members suspect that I am guilty to this very day, claiming that in the end I managed to convince my grandmother to sell the sweeper to Abigail and took a healthy cut for myself. Others believe I sold it on my own and collected the entire sum. I hope that to the reader it is clear that these are false accusations and libelous charges of a most contemptible nature, the kind that only "relations of no blood" can concoct. But there is no longer any chance of convincing those relatives that I am innocent.

At first I tried denial, but that did not work. Then I tried deflecting the accusations onto my cousin Nadav. I said that as he was the last person to visit the bathroom, and the only person to succeed in getting Grandma Tonia to concede to let him use her locked bathroom, nothing would stand in his way and nothing was sacred to him. I noted that he had a clear motive as well: Nadav loves old appliances and, as I have mentioned, is clever with his hands just like his father, Uncle Arik, and our uncle Yitzhak, and shares that inherited love of dismantling and reassembling. He took the sweeper in order to learn its secrets, I claimed. But that did not work, either.

Years have passed and I no longer try to justify or explain or deny, or accuse or slander others. Now even those who still suspect that I am guilty are no longer angry with me; they merely wish I would confess, though not in order to serve justice or because of the money but because they are hungry for another story, another version, another tale.

33

Some months later, on a trip to the United States, I was walking down a street in the endless suburbs of Los Angeles when suddenly my legs stopped moving and stood motionless in the earth like Whitey's hooves before the wadi. I turned around; I had not been mistaken. In the middle of a huge window display of a palatial electrical appliance store there stood—on its own little platform of wood covered in velvet and surrounded by a cohort of modern, state-of-the-art, and brand-new washing machines, dryers, mixers, dishwashers, refrigerators, and vacuum cleaners—Grandma Tonia's sweeper, shiny and preserved.

I drew near and stared. There was no doubt about it: the large rubber wheels, the sparkling chrome canister, the barrel-like size, the thick black tube. And not only had I spotted the sweeper but it had seen me, as well. Gracefully and in silence it rolled forward until it was touching the glass.

I entered the store, expecting to find Abigail at the cash register. But Abigail was not there, nor anyone who could have been her husband or father. There was a salesman, and a cashier, and a manager—perhaps the owner?—a young man, well-mannered and well-dressed.

He asked if I needed help and I asked him where the old vacuum cleaner in the display window had come from.

"It's not for sale."

"I don't wish to buy it," I said, "I just wanted to know where it came from."

He said he had bought it from someone who had picked it up at a garage sale. Then his face softened and he invited me to step into the display window with him.

We went over to the sweeper. "It's like new," he proclaimed proudly. "Mint condition!" He added that there were collectors who would pay at least five thousand dollars for such a "machine of this age and in this condition"—oh, Abigail, how naughty you were!—but he had purchased it for a mere fifty dollars from a guy who had paid twenty for it. "He was even happier than I was. He was sure he'd made a terrific deal.

"It even works," he added. "The only thing it needed was a new sealing ring to replace a damaged one."

My image, reflected in the shiny chrome canister of the

sweeper, was distorted. I looked "vorn down," like someone in desperate need of a spoonful of cream. And more than that: a grandmother who could feed it to me.

"It's a common problem with this model," he noted.

I was relieved. I already looked a lot better, even in the distorted mirror.

"By the way," the man continued, "if you're interested in vacuum cleaners there are a few nice museums in this country. Here in California, too."

"I'm not that interested," I said. "I just stopped in because my grandmother had a vacuum cleaner exactly like this one."

"Interesting," he said. "Why is it that vacuum cleaners of all things can make us so sentimental? Much more than refrigerators or washing machines."

I did not have an answer for that, not to mention the fact that personally I prefer dishwashers.

Sometime later I finished writing my first novel, which described a completely imaginary moshav that had, among other things, a completely imaginary arms cache. In the book I described one completely imaginary woman with a madness for cleaning. In that matter she reminded me a bit of Grandma Tonia, but in spite of all my attempts, she did not hold a candle to her.

I wished to portray this character as a modern witch, and I even wrote a night scene in which she flies through the air, though not on a broomstick but on a vacuum cleaner. I debated myself about where, of all the cities on the glass panel of the radio, she would travel—to Buckingham Palace in London, to the sultan in Istanbul?—but in the end I dispensed those bits to the rubbish bin and decided to stick to the truth: it was not a woman but a donkey that flew to those places. All things considered, even if I am not a true moshavnik, as Uncle Yitzhak once predicted about me, I am still the son of farmers from Nahalal, just as my mother would remind me and repeat often. In other words, I know enough about farming to know that the best fictions of all grow from the earth of reality.

And then what happened? Indeed, the sweeper disappeared and is no longer, much the same as Abigail herself. The beer stein that Grandma Tonia bequeathed me broke. The shed, the laundry house, the chick run, the "excellent shower" in the cowshed, and the cowshed itself have all been destroyed. Grandma's house is rented out to tenants and I have not set foot in it since. The brown headboard of the double bed has become a partition in the calves' pen. That's the way it works in our family: nothing gets thrown away.

Many of the story's heroes have died. Grandma Tonia is no longer, Grandpa Aharon is no longer, and his special citrus tree has been chopped down. Whitey and Ah are no longer, as is true of my mother and father and uncles Moshe, Yitzhak, Yaacov, Binya, Itamar, and, last of all, Menahem. At the time I began writing this book, the family held the first memorial service for him. In some ways it was even more sad and somber than the funeral itself, and produced more crying and sobbing. A torrent of rain fell on the cemetery, adding to the depressing atmosphere. But then his older brother, Uncle Micha, told about a lullaby Grandpa Aharon would sing to Menahem when he was a baby. Aunt Batsheva corrected him at once: "That's not how it was!" she exclaimed, and we all smiled in relief under our umbrellas. In spite of all the deaths, the family is alive, with new versions still being born.

Here ends my story. This is how it was, each version as it is. Because that is how it works with us: we use the language and expressions of the family, and memorize stories, and go nowhere empty-handed, and eat *selyodka,* and the hard-core

211

among us, *kholodich* as well. Because this is what is important: to be loyal to the truth, even if it is not loyal to you; to wring it out wisely, not like a man but like a woman; to tell it in stories and to examine them good good in the light, again and again, until they are as they should be—clear and truly, truly clean.

ABOUT THE AUTHOR

One of Israel's most celebrated novelists, Meir Shalev was born in 1948 on Nahalal, Israel's first moshav. His books have been translated into more than twenty-five languages and have been best sellers in Israel, Holland, and Germany. He is also a columnist for the Israeli daily *Yedioth Ahronoth.* His honors include the National Jewish Book Award and the Brenner Prize, one of Israel's top literary awards, for *A Pigeon and a Boy.* He has been named a Chevalier de l'Ordre des Art et des Lettres by the French government. Shalev lives in Jerusalem and in the north of Israel.

ABOUT THE TRANSLATOR

Evan Fallenberg is the author of the prizewinning novels *Light Fell* and *When We Danced on Water.* He was a finalist for the PEN Translation Prize for his translation of Meir Shalev's *A Pigeon and a Boy.*

A NOTE ABOUT THE TYPE

This book is set in Schneidler, a typeface originally designed for the Bauer Foundry in 1936 by F. H. Ernst Schneidler. Born in 1882 in Berlin, Schneidler is regarded as the founder of the Stuttgart School and recognized as one of Germany's most important twentieth-century typographers and calligraphers. This sturdy and highly readable Venetian-style font is distinguished by even, classical proportions and cupped serifs.

Composed by North Market Street Graphics, Lancaster, Pennsylvania

Printed and bound by Berryville Graphics, Berryville, Virginia

Book design by Robert C. Olsson